BEYOND THE BLANK PAGES

Sam Bell

Kendall Hunt
publishing company

Kendall Hunt
publishing company

www.kendallhunt.com
Send all inquiries to:
4050 Westmark Drive
Dubuque, IA 52004-1840

Copyright © 2016 by Kendall Hunt Publishing Company

ISBN 978-1-4652-8709-0

Printed in the United States of America

CONTENTS

FOREWORD

Here are 27 things to know before reading this book:

1. This book was started in July 2014 after the author wrote an article called "Why Professors Should Give a Damn" for *The Chronicle of Higher Education* that caused a melee in the comments section of the website. The main point of contention was whether instructors bear any responsibility when students perform poorly in class. The author of this book contended that, since learning involves collaboration among instructors and students, they succeed or fail (or some combination of the two) together. Opponents maintained that instructors are simply responsible for providing work for students to do, and for telling students whether they did it well enough. During this discussion, one of the authors of this foreword repeatedly referred to one of those opponents as a "jackass."

2. Sam Bell's idea was simple: treat students as human beings. The public response to this was complex, terrifying, revealing, and hopeful. The response, formal and informal from strangers and friends, was confused or dismissive or condescending or caustic.

3. This (is/is not) a textbook.

4. This book is an exploration of how to write, but it is an exploration of how to live as well.

5. Writing makes sense; it creates order out of chaos.

6. The first part of writing well is just writing. Early in the process, write like you're on fire: fast, frantic, driven by instinct. Step one is getting words on the page. Lots of them.

7. This book blends narrative about the author's own life with advice about writing, thinking, and learning. That's not just the way she writes; it's an illustration of how to make your writing your own: See yourself in it.

8. Textbooks are the children of hornbooks and reference texts.

9. This book should be devoured and retrieved. Hopefully, should this book be found in a library sale with a yellow USED tag on its spine, the reason will be that the former owner had fully absorbed it, as its author hoped.

10. The author is an Emersonian, so do not take her word for it, do it yourself in your own way, but be certain the stones from which you gain momentum are rooted well, or you are likely to confuse slipping with stepping.

11. Truth is not conditional upon stability. Truth is dangerous and disruptive, but so too is thought.

12. The author of this book loves kittens, counting bunnies, allowing the number of bunnies she counts to influence her perception of how good a day it will be, speed-reading true-crime books, and watching the last ten minutes of *The Wonder Years* for a good, therapeutic cry.

13. This book presupposes that you are engaged in your education. If this is not the case, consider why you are wasting your time, energy, and money in a monastic, medieval institution.

14. If you are reading the forward to a textbook, you are among the brilliant and miniscule population that does so.

15. As there are no answers in the back, there are no answers in the front, either.

16. The value of this book depends on you, just as whispering hello is contextual: if you are in the middle of the ocean, it means very little; if you are hiding under your bed, it means something quite different; if you are staring into the love of your life's face, it means something significant. This book is whispering hello to you. How will you respond?

17. Being amenable has its root in the idea of being brought, being prepared to be ready. You need to stretch to be amenable. If you are recalcitrant, you atrophy. If you are amenable, you are poised, prepared, and ready.

18. Aspire to be more than anything offered in an academic setting.

19. "You get out of a class what you put into it" is a treasured cliché among educators. It's as close to true as a cliché can be. Better would be: "What you put into your class you put into yourself."

20. Where we are is not only who we are but how we are as well.

21. All tendrils reach toward chaos. Instability provides movement, reveals essential structures, and disrupts what appears to be stable.

22. Sam's philosophy of education is not born out of an unwillingness to have hard conversations with students or to make unpopular decisions. Hard conversations are the best parts of education. Transactional rigidity is easy.

23. Objective distance is essential to critical thought, and we encourage every writer to strive toward that goal. Though, writing ought to be more than dictation. It ought to be personal. Allow the audience to choose the emotional tone that appeals to their taste, but all writing ought to be personal.

24. An education has to do with vocation, but vocation in its purest form.

25. The value of *Beyond the Blank Pages* is twofold. It serves as a complete document of Sam's educational philosophy, her views on writing, her personal struggles, and her adoration for narrative. Also, it serves as the beginning of a conversation, as narrative ought to be a dialogical experience that includes the readers to engage with what they are reading, and use that as a filter through which to understand what they are seeing.

26. There are plenty of non-jackasses who disagree with much of what this book says about writing, thinking, and learning. There are College Writing Instructors (and others) who think the author's take on the course is overly sentimental and insufficiently rigorous, that the author fails to hold students accountable for the rigorous demands of college work and the world outside academe. Even if they aren't jackasses, those people are wrong. They also, presumably, would not use this book in their classes. If your instructor did choose to use it, that person

likely assumes you are someone whose voice and experiences matter, who has something worthwhile to say, and who deserves support in finding the most powerful ways of saying it. In other words, if your instructor chose this book, you've got one of the good ones.

27. An education is a mask, one that everyone who has experienced school wears. The question is: what mask will you wear? When you read this book, I hope you will ask why. Why do you want to wear the mask of someone disappointed by life? Why does your mask look like someone who's been scolded? Why does your mask demand the admiration of others? Why does your mask look for easy answers or simple solutions? Some of us wear the mask so long it becomes our face. Whatever you do, don't do what you're told to do. Now turn the page.

Ben Stein
Cleveland, OH

Dan McCarthy
Lawrence, KS

ACKNOWLEDGMENTS

This book began because Paul Carty, Executive Editor and Director of Publishing Partnerships at Kendall Hunt, cares about higher education and happened to read my article in *The Chronicle of Higher Education*. It's a special person who reads an article, looks up the author, and asks her if she wants to write a book. Thanks to *The Chronicle of Higher Education* for publishing "Why Professors Should Give a Damn," and thanks especially to Paul for making my dream come true, and for buoying me through this extraordinary experience.

I need to thank my amazing, supportive editor, Senior Development Coordinator Angela Willenbring, for being there for me through the book-writing and beyond. Everyone at Kendall Hunt has made me proud to make this book with them. I am humbled that this team of people, including Coordinator of Higher Education Marketing Ryan P. Brown and Publishing Solutions Representative Leah Fern, have been willing to let this book be what this book needed to be.

I want to thank everyone I work with at Johnson County Community College: these educators are lovely, imaginative, and wonderful people. To the JCCC English Department, and all your glorious encouragement, resistance, support, and vigor to teach the hell out of classes: you are my academic home.

I remember writing a book series when I was seven about people who get stranded on a desert island: I drew a volcano on the cover and bound the stories together to form a staple-spine. I did this because of my mother, my father, my teachers, and Fitzsimmons Dance Factory. I was given a love of creativity from the start and I have been so blessed that I don't even regret having to dress as a real trumpet that one year in tap class, front buttons and all.

Courtesy Samantha Bell

A massive, life-altering privilege I have been given is being part of a family: I love you all.

Mom and Dad: I love you more than the sky and the stars you gave me. You gave me everything. Mom, my closest companion. Dad, my guide.

The educators and teachers I have had: thank you. John Baynes, Gloria Wilner, Cindy Post, Ralph Black, Dave Kelly, Anne Panning, Ken Irby, Mike Johnson, Rachel Hall, Caroline Woidat, Doug Atkins, Mike Valk, Kim Kearney. I am here because of you.

The reason I do most things, at least professionally, is because I love teaching. I love my students. I love that they write to me when they travel, and that we become friends long after classes are over

(Josh, Grant, Drew, Caitlin, Rachel, Ed, Jo, Charles, Mike, Dylan, Mats, Dana, Jen, Helen, Caylin, and so many others—know that I adore you). I will always be grateful to my first class in Rochester at the downtown Monroe Community College campus: you all taught me how to be human, how to watch *American Idol* the proper way, that I wanted to be a teacher, and that I *could* be a teacher.

Where I went to school has mattered greatly to my privileges and opportunities. Fairport, New York has a special place in my heart. Geneseo, New York gave me academic exploration and freedom, and a ton of bad decisions that became really rich material for my first published essays. Geneseo gave me friends like Aria and Caitriona. And Ben Stein. Ben, my brother, my best friend, my husband's best friend, my tormentor of weird mouth sounds, my ethical compass (after college), my family. Ben, I love you very much.

Brockport, New York gave me Rachel, Laura, Palermo, Barber's late nights with Ben and Dan, Joanna McNaney Stein, and Dan McCarthy. Brockport changed everything. Everything: my husband, my friends, my life.

Dan, you're my husband, my confidant, my partner, my best friend, a great Cat Dad, a pretty good singer, a really good chef, and a supporter when I have been sad, scared, or worried, when I have erroneously inflated my sense of self or decided that I do not understand postmodern poetry and that I will have to drop out of graduate school. You are my sun, the grass, this keyboard, my turquoise ring, my sandwich I ate for lunch, my heart. There is no other way to say this. I love you more than anything, even this book. I always will.

Kansas truly is a heartland. Kansas has given me the chance to get my Ph.D. and it gave me the job I have, teaching students. Lawrence, Kansas has given me our neighborhood, our driveway parties, our home that we get to fill with so many beautiful people, Sony Heath and Dannah Hartley: you are our best friends, our chosen family. Kansas has given me the Valks and Valk's pop-ins; you are our family, too. Kansas has given me all our porch sits, all the lunches, all the dinners and kitchen-table cocktails, all the brunches where we tried to think of a title for this book, all the bad reality television and the long visits with Ben, all the phone-dates with Erin and Derek, all your texts asking how the book's going, all the emails about tough days, all the times everyone's been scared of Gus the Cat and his flurry of paws, all the tears, all the celebrations. Goddamn. I love you all so much.

Thanks for reading this, everyone. Thanks for picking up a book about students and higher education and holding it in your hands. Thanks for investigating, pushing academic boundaries, thinking harder, and caring about the work, the students, and who you are a little bit more.

To move deliberately and compassionately is the work of the true educator. Thank you all for showing me the way. xoxo

ABOUT THE AUTHOR

Sam Bell lives in Lawrence, Kansas with her husband Dan and a cat named Gus, as you can see in their lovely family portrait. She is an Associate Professor of English at Johnson County Community College in Overland Park, Kansas. Sam holds two degrees from SUNY schools (B.A., Journalism, Geneseo and M.A., English, Brockport), and a Ph.D. in English from the University of Kansas. Get to know her better at http://sambellgoesnuts.blogspot.com/.

Courtesy Samantha Bell

CHAPTER 1

Finding Yourself in College and in Composition Class

The first college class I ever taught functioned on chaos. People were talking in the back, someone up front was fast asleep, slumped over, someone else had his hand perpetually raised, another was telling a weird news story, and I was in the center, taking notes that were useless on the white board. Chaos: part of the process.

After I got my master's degree at SUNY Brockport, I needed a job. So, I applied to teach at a local community college, Monroe Community College (MCC). I was called in for an interview. It got strange.

My father, on the brink of a breakdown, was trying to stop drinking and wanted to come with me to my interview. This is unusual. Do not let a parent accompany you to a job interview—ever. So, here was my dad in the car, all sweater-vest and khakis, asking me what I was going to say as we drove together to my first teaching interview. He talked the entire ride there. I did not have high hopes.

As we entered MCC's main campus, I ran straight into a guy I went to high school with; I had had the biggest crush on him. I was surprised, and he looked at my dad and me and said, "Hey . . . how are you?" in a pitying way, like a recent development in my life was that I could only go places with my dad. I explained that I was on campus for an interview. He was on his way to a class he was taking. It was a very strange feeling—the first I had in a long string of experiences I see now as Sam-figures-out-her-role-in-the-world. I headed up the stairs, with my father, to wait to be called into the dean's office.

"Stay here," I hissed at my dad in the lounge, praying the administrative assistant did not overhear the woman about to be interviewed for a job shush her father whom she had brought along. When the dean called me in, I put my hand up like a crossing guard: *NO,* to keep my father from coming into the interview with me.

The dean was perfectly pleasant. At the end, he leaned forward, "Why do you think I paused so often as we talked?" I shook my head; I did not know. "To see if you could sit with silence, and what you would do," he said. Later, I understood he was likely referring to the times in class when I would ask a question and no one would answer. That can be excruciating. I got the job.

I was thrilled to be handed a college class to teach. I celebrated with Dan, who was then my boyfriend (he's my husband now), and our best friend Ben. We ate piles of buttered seafood at a restaurant on the Erie Canal and watched it rain. I didn't realize I wasn't a full-time professor. I was an adjunct.

There is so much in college and university life that I did not understand, that is not told to us when we become students and teachers. Someone had to explain to me that adjuncts are paid by the class and get contracts by semester, much like a lecturer at a four-year university. Tenure-track professors, what

I wanted to be, require a full presentation and interview, and a search committee. If you get hired, you become an assistant professor. If you get tenure, you become an associate professor. If you work long enough, you become a full professor. (Currently, I am an associate professor at JCCC). I had thought, that day on the canal, that I had job security. I did not.

What I did have, though, was a class to teach that changed my life. I was 24 when I walked into my first college class as the professor. I was terrified. The class was composed of many **non-traditional students**—students who, for reasons like age and demographic, don't fit into the traditional category of student population (non-traditional usually means things like being age 25 and over, being a single parent, coming back to school after taking a huge break, working a full-time job, etc.). In this class-room, I was one of the youngest. I felt like a non-traditional teacher (too young, too inexperienced, too far-removed from the researched life of a true "academic").

My classroom was at the urban campus, housed in a building in downtown Rochester, NY, that was once a professional series of offices that had shut down; my father had worked in one of the offices, which made the experience of going to class eerie. I had to walk up the no-longer-functioning esca-lator and go through security to get to my class; as a little girl, I remembered Christmas festivities with my mom and dad in this building, me as a little girl, riding in a train car hung from a monorail at the top. I was also sharing an office on the main campus with a former high school English teacher of mine, which was bizarre, given that I thought she had passed away. I had loved her in high school; every time we were in the office together, I felt like a huge imposter, pretending to teach when, really, she was the expert.

I was up against a lot of my own demons.

On the first day of my MCC class, a guy in the front, who I later learned was on methadone, fell asleep, women in the back scoffed when I sat on the desk as the teacher, and a man in the front, a truck driver, made a comment about his daughter being older than me. I was facing a lot of prejudice and assumption. This is a lot like what students can be facing in college. Let me tell you—fight against it with everything that you have.

I told my students about who I was. I told them about my father—that he was unwell and may show up in class (he didn't, but this was, for a bit, a real threat). My father had a habit of showing up at my workplaces, wanting company or to borrow my car. For my students' safety, and my own, I needed them to know about him. They were not fearful; it turned out that they had hosts of their own worries and fears in their lives. I learned about their life concerns largely from their writing.

At the end of every week, we talked about who was winning and who got sent home on *American Idol*. We became a group of people who cared about each other. When one student wrote about the birth of her daughter, I learned it was the only thing she had ever written before. Ever. We processed with a student when his relative was dragged, dead, from the river, or when another student was pulled from class by police. We held each other up.

I tell you this not to set up lofty expectations for the class you are in now. I tell you this because I want you to look around. Who are your people in the classroom? Who are your people on campus? Find them. Talk to them, and listen to them. Show them your writing, and read theirs. The power of an English class resides in the confidence of every writer in the room to tell a story, and to honor it with compassion and an understanding of what that story means. A college education is an education about who you are. Investigate this.

On a late August afternoon in upstate New York, I walked through the quad on the State University of New York (SUNY) at Geneseo's campus. I was thrilled to be there. Everything was green and there were tended gardens and people everywhere. I was with a female student I had just met; we were both freshmen. I thought she was "my people." "My people" at eighteen meant those who dressed up, did their makeup, and made fun of others; this is how I assessed my situation as we walked. The student turned to me, "I just believe in dressing up whenever you're in public, you know? Have some class." I nodded, looking down at my shirt and skirt, and swallowed hard. I thought, *no, no more of this*, while putting on my Sam Bell face of fake perfection.

Turns out, this student was not my people. Let me tell you, it's sometimes hard to find your people in college. And this also means, more importantly, it's hard to find yourself in college. I once had a roommate who wrote me a letter, asking who I actually was. She offered some possibilities: hippie, prep, party girl, dancer, poet . . . I had a hard time discovering who I was in college.

The reason I was walking with the female student who loved dressing up was because I was actively ditching my assigned college roommate. She was purely herself. She loved musicals, laughing, and her boyfriend back home. She was not, I thought, my people, so I put as much distance between her and myself as I could find on the small, beautiful campus. I did a lot of damage doing this—mostly to myself, but also to her.

College became my safe haven. Growing up, I did and did not have a safe home. My father, when he was drinking, was an active alcoholic, and I was an only child. I found safety early on in books and in school. I flourished at people pleasing, and teachers rewarded this. Eventually, I found safety in writing and in English classes. Still, I never thought I would be a teacher or writing this book.

In college, despite my difficulties with personality construction, I fell in love with academic work— not academe as a place, but the work. I loved reading; I loved writing papers; I loved class discussions (though I rarely spoke, likely because I was still finding out who I was). I became an undergraduate teaching assistant (TA) for a creative writing class, and I led discussions about student work—most of whom I went out with on weekends. It was my first experience with being the authority instead of being the student, and I discovered that I liked it more than I thought I would.

Writing can be intimidating, and it might be so for you. That's a wonderful starting place to grow from; if you already know you're good at writing, you have a lovely starting place to dig deeply into what you are capable of. I want to draw an analogy here: writing as planting, and watching what grows, but I would roll my eyes at this, and you would, too. Writing isn't planting. It's an act of self-fulfillment and exploration. Writing is hard work, and that's what makes it rewarding.

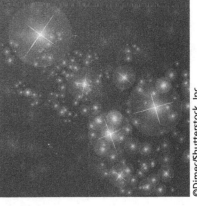

©Dimec/Shutterstock, Inc.

I didn't think I would last one week in the MCC class. When I was observed mid-semester by a colleague, I was sweating through my shirt after fifteen minutes. The class was broken up by bits of unrelated dialogue during discussion. At the end of the observation, when I thought I would get fired, my students stood and clapped for me. I stood and clapped for them, feeling totally overwhelmed. Never forget this: the students, you, are the stars in the room.

You are likely in a Composition I course and have been assigned this book. I want to tell you that it is important that you read this book and pay attention to your professor. But what I need to say is that you matter. Your stories matter, the way you write your life and your thoughts matters, the way you see the world through your language matters. A great class causes you, in any discipline, to re-see things, to reconsider, to open up to newness, and to connect what you learn to other parts of your life. Self-reflection about what you know and how it impacts you is vital to what your education will do for you. Even if (especially if) you resist writing, do a huge favor for Future You and try. Write what you think, write what you know, and ask questions about what you don't know yet. The work of the writer (in and out of a class) is to explore. Try the exercises in this book. Write like your life depends on it (because it does).

At the end of every semester, I write each of my students a letter. I tell each student what I see in them, and I remember things about them that I learned during the semester. They are letters of honest disclosure and, often, celebration. I started this practice after one of my students died (you'll read about this later on), and it stuck. I often come across students after the last class, reading their letters in the hallways. Some cry. Some write me back. I mail the letters to the students who never show back up, or miss the last day. I do this because every single student in my classes matters and needs to know this.

If you are enrolled in a Composition class, I want you to feel fortunate instead of pissed off or frustrated that you have to take this course, because what-am-I-going-to-do-with-this-in-real-life? The answer is everything. Everything in your life is about composition: a movie you watch is composed of the script, actors, music, screenplay, direction, location; how to get on and off the highway is a composition of driving skills, other drivers, street signs, construction, lanes; what you ate today is a composition of manufactured or grown food and what it took to get that food to your mouth. Your decision to go to college right now was composed of many vital factors that got you here. How you communicate and put all your living pieces together will change your life.

I eventually found my words and told that female student at Geneseo that I didn't think we should hang out all the time. I told my roommate I was moving in with other friends next fall. I found my language to help me move in the directions I wanted to be headed when I was in college. And for a while there, I was a mess. And that is okay. I recovered. I found my people. I have since realized that some of my people are those sitting in a classroom: my students. That's a comforting responsibility—it shapes my life and my work. You are my people.

I want to say so many things to you as you start or continue on your path. Instead, I will tell you what my mentor in college did for me, over and over again when I was in class, or when I went to his office hours and he was reading on his office couch, listening to jazz or blues. He would pause, look directly at me, and say, simply, "Hi. How are you?"

Welcome. Stay a while. The whole world is yours. Turn the page.

CHAPTER 2

Analysis and Course Expectations: Yours and Mine

I wrote what I thought was a magnificent paper once, on Salman Rushdie's *The Satanic Verses*. I was convinced the narrator symbolized a third, invisible subaltern identity in the novel, and I used a bunch of literary theorists in an attempt to make my **central focus** (my aim) clear. It was over ten pages long, and I was so proud of tackling a difficult topic in a college class.

Except I had that gut feeling in the pit of my stomach, the one where you know the paper isn't quite focused, clear, or developed, but you are handing it in anyway. Sound familiar? And, the professor had recommended a different topic, one I thought was too pedestrian, when he saw my writing on Virginia Woolf's *Mrs. Dalloway*. I resisted the "easy" topic for one that I thought would impress the professor.

I waited and waited to get that paper back. Finally, we were told to retrieve our papers from the professor's mailbox. I did. I looked at the question marks in the margins on page one. And then, on page two, on the bottom, was this line: *This is where I stopped reading*. My stomach dropped. That was the last mark on the page except for the grade at the end. Grade: C–.

My writing has evolved since then because I took so many writing classes. In college, part of my development was missing as a writer because I never had to take a Composition I course. So, when I was asked to posit an argument about why one communication theory was better than another, I thought that meant to compare them. It didn't. When I was asked to evaluate the merits of feminism in a novel, I thought that meant to find the places where feminism was evident. Not quite. When I was forced to present a speech in my first public speaking course as a freshman, I thought the best way to give an impactful personal speech was to focus on my high school friend who died. Guess what? That speech was way too emotionally driven to be logical, and it wasn't about me. It was about Mike.

I could have used a Composition course to help me in nearly all the coursework that I completed in college. This course offers a skill set made up of **summary, analysis, claims, and conclusions.** You will use this skill set in a combination of ways every day of your life. You might **summarize** (give the overview of) a transaction at work for a colleague. You might make a claim and defend it with evidence (**analysis**) in a relationship. Likely, you will draw important **conclusions** (meanings) about your work, your day, your actions, and your life by day's end.

To **compose** means, simply, to make something new from something already made. Usually, your product is devised from parts of other compositions. It's how toothpaste is made, or the salad you ate for lunch is constructed (good job! It's hard eating healthily in college).

©ANCH/Shutterstock, Inc.

You have been composing all your life, from the time you put syllables together to form words to the time you threw a rad party for your best friend's birthday. The pieces come together to form a new whole.

Usually, when you walk into a Composition class and you are asked why you are there, almost everyone will say, "Because I have to be." Yes, for some programs, especially at a community college, you may need to fulfill this required course to move ahead. The upside is you are attending an institution of learning that cares deeply about supporting your growth as a thinker and as a writer. A Composition class is not a punishment. If it's made to feel that way, consider why—and change that as best you can. Consider investigating your previous educational experiences as a guide for expectations that you have now in college.

Analysis & Education Paper

Steps to consider:

1. Summarize your educational experience before college.

2. Make a claim about your education: was it flawed? How? Was it supportive? In what ways?

3. Find support for your claim. Look at your prior schools' mission statements. Search course outcomes. Interview prior educators. Find out what other students experienced.

4. Make some meaningful conclusions about the significance of your education and how it informs your current life.

Many assume that a Composition course's fundamental goal is to teach you how to write and how to think. In some ways, yes, that is what a Composition course is for. And any other class you take in your life. Your Bio 120 class asks for similar skills in different contexts. Your Fundamentals of Elementary Education course asks you to read, write, and think. I would be surprised to see a course that opposes the basic objective of thinking. Because thinking is an academic goal, Composition I wants to teach you how to think about your thinking. Huh? A major objective in this course should be to process and develop how you form conclusions about a text or idea, how you can apply what you know to a topic, and how to identify what's unknown about a topic for further exploration. This course wants you to consider thoroughly how you reach conclusions instead of assuming that making conclusions, forming a thesis, or analyzing a text come naturally. They're learned skills. It's like merging onto a highway: you know how to drive the car, but you need additional skills to merge safely into a lane.

So. You have to write and you have to think. Not too bad, right? At this point are you wondering why this course differs from any other and why you have to take this specific one? Are you bored, annoyed, hungry, angry? Do you have better things to do?

You might be hungry. Take a break. But you do not have better things to do. I spent a lot of my undergraduate college career thinking I was above certain classes. I wasn't. I needed skills to read better, to look harder, to analyze more precisely, to explain, support, and defend claims. This class will help you with these pieces of your education, and you can apply them to the world you will inhabit.

Educators in America have big ideas about what a Composition class is supposed to include and what students like you are supposed to perform. Before we handle these course expectations from a national level, I want you to consider what will be the most important piece of this course:

What do you want out of this course?

When I ask my students this, they say, *An A. Fine*, I usually say, *but what is an A*? How do you gain one? What does that entail?

Your Personal Composition I Course Expectations Exercise

If you can move beyond a grade as your highest aspiration (and that's difficult, but not impossible, I promise), take a minute and process a few critical questions about this course.

Your answers will dictate your level of expectation, and thus engagement, in this class. Why? Because despite what you are asked to write, in each moment of composition, you are able to work on your own skill set. The issue is being aware of that skill set while writing, speaking, and composing.

Question 1: What do you want to gain from this course in relationship to your writing skills?

Question 2: Why, aside from requirements, will you stay enrolled in this course? (What will make you consistently attend and stay engaged?)

Question 3: How do you currently communicate, and what needs to change about that?

Question 4: Do you privilege content, ideas, organization, or mechanical clarity most when you write a paper?

Here's an example. Years ago, in a Composition I class, I assigned a narrative document to be composed that made meaning out of a struggle, conflict, or challenge the student had endured. The mode of composition was individual. You, as a student, could write an academic paper, make a film, create a photo essay, conduct and edit interviews for an audio file, etc. One student wanted to describe his experiences being in the foster care system and eventually becoming adopted. To do this, he had to explain his upbringing, his father's drug use, and his foster families in and around central Kansas City.

This student was overwhelmed by writing a paper because the amount of material he had to describe was huge for him. He also believed that, while he needed help with grammar, he wanted to advance his communication skills as a speaker.

Thus, the option of composing a film was born. The student interviewed members of his foster family. He **narrated** (told his personal experience from his own point of view) his own story as we saw streaming images of places where he had lived prior to his adoption. In the end, he spoke honestly about his experiences and why they were meaningful in narration.

The film, once edited, cut, and revised for organization, was an incredibly moving document that, yes, satisfied the A grade, and, more importantly, demonstrated what a successful set of Composition I expectations can be. The film supported the basic tenets that the National Council of Teachers of English (NCTE) agree upon for what a Composition I class should be.

Nationally, the NCTE, in conjunction with a committee of members from the Conference of College Composition and Communication (4Cs), produces guidelines for a standard, successful college Composition I class and these become implemented at colleges and universities throughout America. I will briefly show you some of their expectations of this course. Then, we have to talk about them and analyze them to make them meaningful to your life as a student and individual.

The Conference on College Composition and Communication (4Cs)'s Position on What Postsecondary College Writing Should Accomplish

- Emphasize the rhetorical nature of writing (have the ability to recognize multiple purposes and expectations of a written work)

- Consider the real audience for the work

- Accept that writing is a social act

- Analyze material and practice writing in a variety of genres (types of writing)

- See the writing process as iterative and complex (using a standard grammar to express ideas)

- Emphasize the relationships between writing and technology

- Support learning, engagement, and critical thinking

Our initial aim now is to analyze these guidelines. Do you understand them? Can you achieve them? What's missing? What's less useful to you? Can you define what is meant by writing is a "social act"? Can you defend or criticize how you support learning, engagement, and critical thinking in this class?

If we return to the student film, we can see that the student achieved success with these guidelines because he had outcomes in mind. He had a dual purpose, which was to explore his upbringing and to show his strength in surviving. His real audience was known. He knew he would show this film to people—that's the basic expectation of a film. He utilized interviews, script, mechanical clarity in captions, and narrative genres for his film. He maintained a consistent tone throughout his narrative and his grammatical choices were also constant. He clearly showed **synthesis**, the act of combining, by unifying technology, audio recording, photography, and narrative writing in the film. By investigating his past, he naturally learned about his experiences, who he was, and where this past could support his future goals as an entrepreneur in his community. All this was accomplished because he took the reins of his assignment and made it his.

The fundamental purpose of a Composition I class—what you should expect—is that it is a site of discovery. Some discover more about why their pasts have shaped who they are. Some discover they are great at editing material. Some discover that grammar makes sense to them. Whatever the discovery is, it matters, and it will enhance the experiences you have in subsequent courses.

Here's a series of identifiers about what you value more in your own writing that will help you determine what you want to get out of this class.

Student Identifiers for Course Outcomes

Identifier 1. On the scale below, place an X to indicate which outcome you value more: assessing your writing's rhetorical nature and purpose, or writing new original content in a document. The X is neutral.

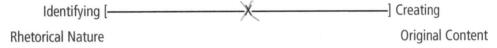

Identifying [————————————X————————————] Creating

Rhetorical Nature   Original Content

Identifier 2. On the scale below, place an X to indicate which outcome you value more: writing as a social act, or using correct grammar. The X is neutral.

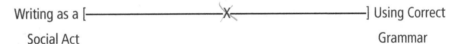

Writing as a [————————————X————————————] Using Correct

Social Act   Grammar

Identifier 3. On the scale below, place an X to indicate which outcome you value more: using technology, or developing critical thinking. The X is neutral.

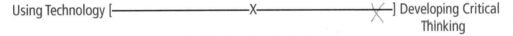

Using Technology [————————————X———————————X—] Developing Critical
                                                                                    Thinking

What are your answers? If you fall in the middle, or close to neutral on all three, you are a prime candidate to soak up everything you can in this course.

If you lean more toward valuing creating original content, writing as a social act, and developing critical thinking, then exploring and writing new material is a theme for you in this course. You will want to take as much charge as possible of the topics and outcomes of your writing assignments. Do this as much as you possibly can, because your writing and thinking skills will grow. If, say, you lean more toward valuing identifying your rhetorical nature, using correct grammar, and using technology, you will spend a lot of time narrowing your audience and purpose as you revise and edit your work. Together, all the students in this class will have a mix of these results, which means peer editing, class discussions, and group work will benefit from your specific skill sets as the semester progresses. Do not waste these skills you can offer. Use them during the semester to develop your writing strengths, and share them in class to model the important skills you have.

The Council of Writing Program Administrators (CWPA) has, in alignment with the 4Cs Composition I expectations, produced a small list of what students should be capable of in the course. In a lot of ways, this is what college professors believe are the core values, or core expectations, or learning outcomes, for you. Here they are:

Composition I Core Learning Outcomes

According to the CWPA, in this course, you will:

- Develop voice, tone, and understanding of an appropriate level of formality in your work

- Find, evaluate, analyze, and synthesize material

- Understand that language is connected to knowledge and power

- Understand how your ideas relate to a larger concept or someone else's work

---

This is not a comprehensive list. Generically, these outcomes are meant to be dropped into any Composition I course and manipulated to fit the needs of the course, institution, and professor. That's good. Still, return to what you want and deserve out of this course. What are your student learning outcomes for yourself?

This process of naming your own student learning outcomes matters a great deal—and not just because you or someone you love or the government is paying for this course. You are spending valuable time, energy, and thought on any production of work in this course. Making your time valuable is a skill that will allow you to be an asset at a job, in a family system, in your relationships. Your own outcomes can be whatever you want them to be. Here are a few student outcomes that often get overlooked:

Overlooked Student Outcomes

- Expect to be respected and not offensively judged in this course

- Expect to be handled with dignity and grace

- Expect to be given the space to question and challenge lectures and theories presented to you

- Expect to be offered campus resources when you need them

- Expect to have the freedom to explore assignments in innovative ways

- Expect to be heard

Now, what can you add to this list for yourself and your classmates?

This process of naming, and adhering to, your student learning outcomes also matters because it will allow you to re-frame class discussions, will give you richer content to discuss with your professor, and will allow you to advocate for yourself when you have a vision for a specific assignment.

If you determine, adhere to, and communicate your own outcomes in this course, your work will improve. This also matters because you have a professor in class who, likewise, has expectations for you.

My basic expectations of a student in a Composition I course are fairly simple—or, rather, they are focused on the human experience of being a person in a room full of people.

Basic Expectations of a Student in a Composition I Class

- Turn off your phone. Please, please stop texting during class. It's like a giant electronic whisper that won't stop and I am distracted when I see it happen.

- Attend class.

- Treat everyone with the same high level of respect.

- Hear others in conversation and do not interrupt.

- Let other people speak.

- Write with risk.

- Do not plagiarize old papers as if your narrative has not changed since high school. That's boring.

- Believe in yourself. If a teacher has never said you are worthwhile, consider this: I am saying this to you. Believing in yourself makes a lot of difference.

Some professors care a great deal about the quality of your work. I do, too. I'm often told that I am a difficult grader. That's because I want you to be as expressively accurate as possible, or as persuasive, or as unbiased, in the writing and work you create—because if you can accomplish this here, you will keep reaching this level of quality communication elsewhere.

Beware anyone who does not constructively criticize. **Constructive criticism** is when your evaluator sees positive elements *and* pieces to work on. Both should be identified. Writer Roxane Gay told the *New York Times Magazine* that her dissertation's central focus was investigating if faculty members fetishize the idea that students are bad writers. She studied how often professors complained about your "bad writing." She found that faculty wanted to complain more than they wanted to be right: the evidence points to your writing as being good, strong, worthwhile. The complaining was determined to be the problematic behavior, not the quality of the student writing. Beware a complainer. Challenge the complainer. Ask for positive criticism.

You are the reason the class is held. Without students, the class is empty. Make it yours, and meet with your professors when that isn't happening. Explain, in evidence-based analysis, what is and is not working well. I wish I had asked my professor for feedback on the remaining eleven pages of unmarked text. Instead, I let fear take over. This is your class, and your writing. You deserve an experience beyond the "gut" course, beyond the blank pages. Make it so.

©Alex Andrei/Shutterstock, Inc.

SUGGESTED MATERIALS

American Association of Community Colleges. "Students at Community College." 2014. Web.

Link: http://www.aacc.nche.edu/AboutCC/Trends/Pages/studentsatcommunitycolleges.aspx

Conference on College Composition and Communication (CCCC). "Principles for the Postsecondary Teaching of Writing." *NCTE.org.* 25 Nov. 2013. Web.

Link: http://www.ncte.org/cccc/resources/positions/postsecondarywriting

Council of Writing Program Administrators. "WPA Outcomes Statement for First Year Composition." *WPAcouncil.org.* 17 July 2014. Web.

Link: http://wpacouncil.org/files/WPA%20Outcomes%20Statement%20Adopted%20Revisions%5B1%5D_0.pdf

Gay, Roxane. "Roxane Gay's 'Bad' Feminism." *The New York Times Magazine* 25 July 2014. *nytimes. com.* Web.

Link: http://www.nytimes.com/2014/07/27/magazine/roxane-gays-bad-feminism.html?_r=0

Your Institution's English Department Student Learning Outcomes and Course Outline.

CHAPTER 3

Relationships and Language: The Power of Composing

It was a late summer evening and I was with my boyfriend, Dan, at a BBQ thrown on the lawn of one of our graduate school professors. Standing there, looking at the sun going down, I quickly realized that Dan and I should get married. Neither one of us believed in the virtue of marriage as a social construct at the time, but I remember standing on that green grass as the BBQ was winding down, staring at Dan laughing. I held a glass of wine in my hand; Dan was across the yard with a friend, talking with his hands, beer bottle waving around, and the sun was gently working its way below the roofline. I loved him. He loved me.

We walked home, through the main drag in town, decided to get a beer at a tavern that was perched on the canal. We made our way to the patio where boats crept by, headed for home.

"I want to get married," I blurted.

Dan's face was openly surprised; freckles jumped off his face, startled, and ran into the canal.

We fought about it, in public, on this lovely end-of-summer eve. The fight ended with me shouting, as I was preparing to stomp off, "Either you marry me or we have to break up."

That isn't even logical. And, more to the point, the words I was meaning were not the words I was saying.

Has this ever happened to you? You say something ridiculous, knowing it's not exactly what you mean, but you cannot take it back and now the mending of your stupid words requires more words to mend it completely?

Have no fear—the mending will happen if and when you get your words back. When I mended this situation, Dan and I decided we would eventually get married. We had an important talk. And we did get married, about a year later.

Welcome to Composition I: the course that should teach you how to compose, communicate what you mean, and not do what I did.

As we've already discussed, composing is working with pieces to make a new whole. This course is, yes, a writing course. I prefer to see it as a course about language, a course that privileges word choice as an intentional, thoughtful act of communication.

COMPOSITION means, throughout a project, identifying several key elements

    FOCUS means what the thesis, anchor, or central idea of the work is

What is the center of the work? For me, when I write about demanding that Dan marry me, the center is just that: I foolishly misused my language and miscommunicated what I meant, which was that I wanted to spend my life with Dan. What is your primary goal with your work? If I keep writing about this scene with Dan, my goal is to prove that I loved Dan, and that sometimes, language gets screwy when we mean for it to be direct. Mixed messages cause consequences we have to work through. For you, whatever the focus is, make sure it appears in all areas of your work—all paragraphs, all images, all scenes. The focus is also seen as the **rhetorical nature of the work**, or its purpose. Find a deeper, more significant reason to create the work. This is where the **So What?** question emerges. Ask yourself why your work matters—it does, and have an answer. Mine is to show, with the BBQ and subsequent bar scenes, how language can be misused and why that's important in relationships. In your own work, have an answer about why your topic matters.

    AUDIENCE means who will read, hear, or see the work

Identify very clearly who the work is for beyond the person grading it. If you write a speech for high school students, do you mean general high school students in America? Middle-class students in Georgia? What kind of student populations are you trying to reach? If you make a film for government officials about your city's recycling program, what do you want the officials to see and do? Get clear on your audience right away, because what you want your audience to know and do shapes how you create. My audience for writing about Dan is college-aged individuals and up, those who likely have experience with the complexities of romantic relationships and choices about marriage.

    FORMAT or **MODE** means what type of document you will create now that you have identified the focus, audience, and rhetorical nature of the project

Like my student who made a digital narrative on film in chapter two, you may have a choice about the formats of your semester projects. You might have the choice to create a **multimodal work** (a work using more than one form, such as photographs paired with written research, or a film with narrative overlay) or a single-mode work (a work using one form, such as a written essay). Multimodality is common with technology available to us. Instead of writing a paper, consider, for example, filming your family and making a **digital narrative** out of it (a film rendition of a personal story), or a **photo essay** (a collected group of photographs and corresponding text). All the work here begins with the power of word choice and knowing what type of document will best accomplish your goal.

    DETAILS means all the important main ideas, descriptions, and necessary information about the topic

What can you tell us, show us, describe to us, that is necessary for the purpose and focus of the work? Be specific. If your photo essay takes place in the Midwest, tell me if we're in Kansas or Missouri, etc. If your purpose is to persuade people in your town to adopt more animals from the Humane Society, give evidence to answer the So What question, and then explain all the steps to make the adoptions happen.

AUTONOMY means the ability to control your project

Economist Dan Pink calls autonomy one of the greatest motivators for success. If you have as much control as possible over all aspects of a project in this course, your work will be of exponentially higher quality because your choices have meaning to you.

You will also need **introductions** (beginnings) and **conclusions** (endings), but these will differ depending on the type of document you are creating. For example, if you are developing a concept in a photo essay, you may choose to forego a written introduction because you want the viewer to make inferences and discoveries about what the viewer is seeing in a gradual manner. Your choices about how to begin and how to end a text all come down to being able to know your focus, develop it, satisfy the audience's expectations (and your own), and cover all your bases—leave no scene or example out when it helps the goal of the project.

Back to my own example. I started this chapter by describing a scene with images so you could see it. My hope is that my level of detail puts you into the moment, introduces Dan and me, and sets the scene to unfold. In the middle, I would develop more scenes to explain the fallout from my demand that Dan marry me or leave me. I would likely show you even more examples of when I kept using inarticulate language and suffered consequences for it, such as when I miscommunicated how I wanted my hair colored to my hair stylist the night before my first day of teaching began, and, to comfort me, Dan told me I looked like *The Blair Witch Project*, thinking this would soothe me. I would then conclude with how Dan and I resolved our disputes and got married, and how my hair color went back to normal.

Most students come into my class thinking that they will only be writing papers. Often, they are bored by writing prescriptive papers. I give guidelines for each unit project, and I also give options. In this way, the students' autonomy is preserved and the guidelines are able to help structure, focus, and enrich the choices the students make.

Writing an Autonomous Project

When you are assigned an autonomous project, it's common to feel overwhelmed. Instead, ground yourself by moving through these choices.

Participants: Will you work in a group? With a partner? Alone?

Topic: What will the topic be? Why? Answer the "So What" question. If you don't have an answer, try talking it through. Okay. I want to write about that time when I told Dan he either had to marry me or he had to break up with me. So what? Well, it showed me that language matters, and so does logic, because he got really mad, and also confused. He didn't think I wanted to get married. Aha. This is about language choices. That matters to everyone who has relationships and uses language in them because language affects the quality of our relationships.

Continued

> **Purpose:** What is the purpose of the project? How will it be seen, read, heard? See the paragraph above. If you can determine why your topic matters, you have your purpose.
>
> **Mode:** What format will this take?
>
> **Audience:** Determine who should see or hear your project, and who will benefit from this project.
>
> **Outcome:** What is your final goal, or outcome, with this project? Aim for this.

The point of composing is to learn that language and images are powerful. We know this emotionally from interacting with others. But bringing this power into a classroom is valuable work. For example, I hid my battle with anorexia when I was asked to write about how I connected to texts in English classes. I didn't disclose my history with anorexia until I was a senior in college, and, by then, my writing skills had developed in the range of analysis and evaluation of a subject—I had gotten good at masking true material by **intellectualizing**, or writing *around* my disorder, not *about* it. By the time I was challenged in a creative writing workshop to write a narrative nonfiction essay, it was like I was re-learning how to write. I was not asked to analyze the dysfunctional behavior of anorexics in general. I was charged with writing about my starvation and to describe, in detail, my ongoing disease. Had I tried this type of honest writing earlier in my college career, this experience would not have been so frightening. I finally wanted to explore these pieces of my life. I needed to figure out how and why.

Composing means communicating because when we select words to use, and put them in order, or when we select images and show these to an audience, we're attempting to connect to the audience. For example, when a student in class was exiting an abusive relationship, she realized that her persuasive writing and fact-based writing in class improved her ability to fill out the necessary forms for a restraining order, along with preparing her to compose a statement at a trial with her abuser. The more articulate she was, the safer she became.

The ways in which we compose, or write, think, show images, and make conclusions, have the opportunity to change lives. When I began writing about my life through narrative, I grew more confident in my ability to talk to others, particularly during job interviews. Once I saw that I could articulate my experiences and why they were meaningful, I was able to talk specifically about my skills, strengths, and weaknesses.

There are many ways in which your language shapes you, your experiences, and the power you have over or with these experiences. If, say, you need to ask for a day off at work, how will you compose this request? In person? In email? In a text? Which one is appropriate? It depends on the context of your relationship with the person who may or may not grant you permission for the day off.

If you're fighting with your friend, and you text her, and she wanted you to call her instead, your composition choice has missed its mark, and possibly done damage. How many of you have received a message in a less personal mode than you would have wanted? A Facebook message from a personal friend, voicing concern about you skipping classes? *Why didn't she talk to me*, you might think. A phone call from a friend you haven't seen since first grade? Is that welcome or uncomfortable? We make composition choices daily, and then we make language choices to make our messages as clear as possible.

Exercise

Try to discover some of your composing preferences, along with types of writing that come most naturally to you. Next to each subject below, name the mode (type) of communication you would use to communicate a message (such as a phone call, an email, a text, a letter, a paper, etc.) and jot down a brief message of what you would say or write.

Subject: Giving bad news to a good friend

   Mode: *One-on-one conversation in person*

   Message:

Subject: Asking a college professor for an extension on a major assignment

   Mode: *Email*

   Message:

Subject: Asking a relative for money

   Mode: *Email*

   Message:

Subject: Following up on a job application

   Mode: *In-person meeting*

   Message:

Subject: Having to create a capstone (final) academic project in your area of interest

   Mode:

   Message:

Circle any mode that occurs more than once. What might this say about your choice of composing a message?

Next, choose one of the subjects that is, or could be, a true event in your current life, and write out what you would say. Actually compose this message to the chosen person.

Subject: Talking to parents about parent visitation weekend.

Mode: Email

Written Message: I've looked at some of the scheduled options, and I definitely agree that it would be nice to go to the welcome dinner boat cruise. I don't know what time you two are arriving, but I would like to go to the duck boat tour and the marine science center if at all possible...

Look at your sentences. Are your sentences long? Descriptive? Short? Terse? What kind of **tone**, or emotional value, are you displaying? Do you focus more on the issue, yourself, or the person? Do you stick to the present or bring up the past or future? Do you soften the message? Make the message direct? All these identifiers tell you a wealth of information about how and in what ways you are comfortable composing.

After moving through the work we do in a Composition I class, I hope you will have composed in ways that have challenged you and that have shown you where your written, rhetorical, and compositional skills are strongest. All this means is that you will be able to identify what type of writing fits any context, use your writing strengths, and anticipate what is necessary to fully communicate your message to a specific audience. This is where power comes in. How? By choosing the appropriate mode and message, you communicate powerfully. This helps you survive, gain employment, enrich relationships, save time, and advocate for yourself.

When I finally figured out how I wrote most powerfully, which was with honest narrative about my own experiences, my life became clearer to me. When I was able to write about my anorexia with clarity and direct, clear language that showed and disclosed my skeletal self, the world opened up for me. I was less fearful of being judged, and I was more fortified in my recovery. That's what I want for you in this course: to discover the ways in which composing and using language can shape your life in powerful ways, ways that fortify who you are and who you are capable of becoming, like saying, "I do," when you're ready and able to do so.

©Brian Goodman/Shutterstock, Inc.

SUGGESTED MATERIALS

Baile, Brian. "'If You Don't Believe that You're Doing Some Good with the Work that You Do, then You Shouldn't Be Doing It': An Interview with Cindy Selfe." *Composition Forum* 21, Spring 2010.

Link: http://compositionforum.com/issue/21/cindy-selfe-interview.php

Elliott, Stephen. "Where I Slept." *The Rumpus.net.* 1 Apr. 2009.

Link: http://therumpus.net/2009/04/where-i-slept/

The New York Times. "One in Eight Million." Digital Storytelling Site. 2014.

Link: http://www.nytimes.com/packages/html/nyregion/1-in-8-million/

Pink, Dan. "The Puzzle of Motivation." TED Talk. Aug. 2009.

Link: http://www.aacc.nche.edu/AboutCC/Trends/Pages/studentsatcommunitycolleges.aspx

Stanton, Brandon. *Humans of New York.* Photo Essays. 2010-ongoing.

Link: http://www.humansofnewyork.com/

CHAPTER 4

Writing Narratives: The Story of You

My father is a recovering alcoholic. There, I wrote it. When I was growing up, he drank orange soda mixed with vodka, wine with dinner, beer on Saturday afternoons. Is this opening interesting enough for you to keep reading?

I hope so.

The reason **narratives**, or focused stories about parts of our lives, compel us to read more is because human lives and human experiences are usually interesting, and for two significant reasons:

1. We're curious how other people's lives are so vastly different from our own.

2. We are seeking help, reassurance, and guidance from those who have experienced events that mimic our own in some way, usually tragically.

Often, when I ask students at the beginning of the semester to write about their pasts, they groan. *Why?* I ask them. *Because*, they say, *I am not interesting*.

Aha, *but you are,* I say back. You've just been living your own life this whole time, so you know what happens next.

What happened next with my father's narrative is any reader's guess. If you have had an alcoholic parent, relative, or friend, you might have a more educated guess. But no one can specifically know what happened to get my father into recovery unless I write the next section of that story.

STORY. Is a narrative a story? Yes, without a doubt, a narrative has to act or we're bored, because a narrative cannot be a summary. Have you ever had someone in your own life who tells you every moment of her day, summing up everything her teachers wore, what she thought of her chicken sandwich, the way her boyfriend sounded when he called? What usually happens? You stop listening.

The goal of a narrative is to keep the audience listening, on the page and in speech, because you have meaningful things to say and write, and because you want to share them with your audience. Connecting your life events, for you, helps make sense of the world, which is true **analysis** (making conclusions and meaning from observation). Connecting your life to others' lives in writing is what makes us human.

Your key to a narrative is its focus. When you write a **personal essay**, which is a narrative essay about a specific piece of your life, you have to decide the focus, or the reason for telling the story. Will your personal essay be about your history of being a long-distance runner? Then being a long-distance runner will be your focus. Will you write a narrative about your first car accident? If so, the accident, and its impact on you, is the focus. All the pieces of your narrative, or personal essay, will revolve around the focus. Determine this and move out from here.

When writing a narrative, your choices are huge because you have a big, long life already lived. You will need a **central focus**, something I call an **anchor**. A central focus is what ties all your paragraphs and details together; some call this a **thesis**. Select a focus. Mine, so far, is how my father's drinking affected my childhood. Now, remember how long your focus took to emerge and develop in your actual life. Was it a singular moment in time? Was the focus developed over a span of time?

Once you have a focus, determine its timeline. Here are some timelines to choose from:

1. A single event: you have the time leading up to the event, the event, and the recovery from the event, such as what led up to your car accident, what happened during the accident, and how you recovered and were impacted by the accident afterward.

2. A span of time when the focus was happening: you have the year your dad was in rehab, or the months when you were depressed, or the basketball season where you played well.

3. Fragmented, connected times: you have all the times, throughout your life, when the same thing happened, such as all the times your family went on vacation and you broke a bone, all the ages when you struggled with math, all the school years when you made the cheerleading team. Pick and choose the most relevant.

After selecting the timeline and the focus, you will soon become aware that your narrative has an **audience**. Your audience in narrative is a big deal because you might be afraid that the audience will judge you. Even if you say, *no, they won't*, or I *don't care*, usually we care at the end of the day about what we have been told and by whom. Your audience should be determined by you: would this narrative be better read by teenagers? College students? In this academic setting, select an audience who doesn't know you—this causes you to fill in gaps with significant details and avoids you relying on personal shared history with the reader.

Having an audience of strangers creates tension because you are in charge of your reputation in the narrative. This does not mean you should restrict your narratives to stories of you being heroic, saving dogs and babies and being the best son ever. That gets old after a while because, as humans, we also do this: we doubt perfect stories. And we should because, even if you did save that baby, you have more of the story to tell. Where you were coming from, or why you were there, or how did you know to save the baby when no one else in the mall did? All these pieces configure into parts of the story.

The professors you give your narratives to might assign specific topics for guidance, such as a **literacy narrative** about how you learned to read and write, or a **family of origin narrative** where you define and describe your own family system. My advice is to construct as much of a meaningful narrative as possible surrounding the focus. The textures and details of the experiences you have had leading up to and coming away from your central focus make the narrative succeed or fail. And let's be honest, no one wants his own narrative to fail. You matter. Your story matters.

The point of a good narrative is not at all to write an **autobiography**. Do not write an autobiography. Really, no one will read an autobiography because it must be distinct from the narrative for a specific reason: an autobiography must chronicle your entire life. Write a focused narrative instead that is unified by a **theme**.

Because you are writing a narrative which is a focused bit of writing, develop your focus by locating a **theme**. It likely has one already, even if you don't see it yet. A **theme** is simply the connective tissue that supports and develops the focus. For example, let's say your narrative's focus is about transferring to a new high school when you were 15. The focus is the transferring; the theme is how social you became. Explore the theme by showing examples of making friends, joining the basketball team, and going to parties on weekends (if this is your story to tell).

Finding themes is not as difficult as what we're taught. We make connections all day, every day.

To find a theme, I advise this simple series of steps. You can do this in class or as a brainstorming practice on your own.

A Theme Identification Exercise

Step 1: Make a list of all the things, people, beliefs, possessions that you value.

Step 2: Circle your top five values.

Step 3: Rank your top five values from highest to lowest:

Highest:

Second:

Third:

Fourth:

Lowest:

Step 4: Re-read the top five rankings. What connects them? What do they share in common?

Find a connection. It might take time, but there is one. This connection, what ties your top five values together, is a theme. Your top five values could be individual paragraphs that develop the theme. Once written, the focus is what connects the top five values, the big picture (for example, family). The theme is what the top five values signify (family, for example, is very important to your identity).

The point here is to start the process of investigating who you really are. The more you can identify who you are and why you got to be this person, the more confident you will be in all areas of your life, from job to home to student. Being confident takes a great amount of risk. In a lot of ways, we are taught not to write too much about ourselves or too vividly about challenging topics. But the challenging topics make up who we are as much, or more, as the easier topics to disclose. If, say, you went to prison and believe this is the anchor for your narrative, you have to write that narrative; you are now required to tell us how you got to prison, what prison was like, and what happened since you were released. A solid prison narrative, and there are many, such as John Edwards' "Prison Man Considers Turkey," or Larry Smith's "A Life to Live, This Side of the Bars," tell us how the subject arrived in prison and what happened in prison. Without explanations, all of us watching *Orange Is the New Black* would be in a state of perpetual anger and question-asking. Fill in the gaps.

If I casually, in my narrative, disclose that someone in my life cheated on me, and go on to describe my lack of trust with men in general, you are likely still wondering about the someone who cheated on me. Who was it? The point here is, once you drop someone or something into your narrative, you have to deal with him, her, or it. You cannot pretend they are not lurking, begging for explanations. A way around this is to omit the drop-in, but be aware, this changes the text surrounding the omission. Now we're left wondering more generally why I don't trust men (this is not true, I do trust most men), pre-supposing that something must have happened to make me distrust men (it did). We need explanations and moments in our narratives to fill in the gaps. Otherwise, we fill in your narrative gaps with our own life experiences. And filling in the gaps from our own lives is dangerous, risky, because it is not achieving accuracy. We're staring at our own stories, not yours. Always, always bring the reader back to your story.

You can also take risks with a positive approach to your narrative. Let's say you want to write about your decision to become an elementary school teacher. You are going to have to tell us why. And that will require, for a successful narrative, events, moments, and memories of you perhaps experiencing alternative career choices that you were not good at, and definitely experiencing specific moments with children that counted. Make us see these moments and we'll root for your teaching career to work out.

When you have to write a narrative for your Composition class, there are some common reactions: *No,* or *I already did one in high school*, or *I don't have anything to write about*, or *This is too overwhelming and I hate this class.*

First, don't say no. People who are scared say no. I get that you are scared. That's awesome. Stay here for a while. There's an exercise coming up that will help you.

If you already wrote a narrative in high school, get it out and look at it, carefully. Look at the word choice, emotional maturity, and choices made in the text. What did you write? Look carefully enough to identify changes you have made already in your life, or look at what has stayed because your identity has a solid, pretty airtight theme already.

You have something to write about if you are alive.

And the hate. If you hate this class or this narrative assignment, pay attention in two ways:

1. Why do you hate writing about yourself? Find an answer to that (often, what you're avoiding *is* the focus of your narrative if you can get to that honest place of acceptance).

2. Use the resistance to know that you prefer non-narrative types of writing. That's okay. There are more writing types to come.

If you struggle with starting a paper (and who doesn't?), try this approach to a narrative.

Memory-Keeping Exercise

Step 1: In five minutes, write a specific, singular memory you have from ages 1–10.

Step 2: In another five minutes, write a completely new, specific, singular memory from ages 11–15.

Step 3: Take five more minutes, and write a completely new, specific singular memory from ages 16–today.

Step 4: Re-read all three memories.

Step 5: What age range stands out as most vivid? Why?

Step 6: What ties the three memories together? This is your theme.

Step 7: Where and when do all three memories take place? Do all three memories take place in the afternoon, or in Kansas, or when you felt scared? (Where and when are they happening?)

Step 8: What memory could you expand upon?

For some, this exercise will become a draft of a focused narrative. If you have identified a focus or a theme, you are on your way.

Once you begin writing a narrative, you have to choose and revise pretty seriously to make the content informative and vivid. You do not want too much **summary**. Summary is necessary for plot points and geography: who were you with, where were you, what time of day, what age, what state, what time? Once the summary is given, move into necessary **background** when it arises.

Background is not summary. Background is necessary detailed information that outsiders need to know to understand your plot points. For example, if I summarize my dad's drinking life, I can tell you that my dad drank a lot at home on weeknights in upstate New York where we lived. Okay. If I want to give you background, I can tell you that my dad started drinking before dinner when I was a kid. I remember him always having a drink before dinner, wine with dinner, and another drink after dinner, then another. I can tell you that almost every night, he complained about dinner, and it was because he was already drunk. I can tell you that I was usually quiet at the table so he wouldn't yell.

All those background details help give an indication of what my dad, as a drinker, was like because you weren't there to witness these experiences. If I write that my dad drank a lot with Lee, you have no idea who Lee is. Lee is my mother's younger brother, my uncle. That is necessary background information to move the story along. Don't let your readers fill in your gaps with their own lives. Show and describe enough to let them see what you see in memory.

Then, you need to balance this background with details. Show body language, gestures, and facial expressions. Give time of day, season, the sound of someone's voice, the length of someone's hair. My dad, for instance, is six feet tall, with brown hair, glasses, and an impeccable sense of formal dress. The collar on his Polos is always buttoned to the top, and always pink or yellow. These details matter. You wouldn't want to be the faceless wonder in someone else's narrative, so make sure you don't draw stick figures in your own.

Courtesy Sam Bell.

Once you have a focus, a theme, and a reasonable amount of details, add scenes to show events that happened, such as the time when my dad drank too much and fell into the framed artwork in the downstairs hallway. Glass went everywhere. If possible, include conversations in actual dialogue. Here is where writers get nervous. They ask if they can really recount a conversation because they don't remember it word for word. *Isn't that unethical*, people ask. Yes and no.

If you are someone who fully believes in the virtue of specificity and accurate writing, well, that's going to be a nearly impossible road. If you are among the rest of us who have shades and lines of gray in our mostly true stories, you can approximate your conversations. I suggest writing dialogue line by line, because it reads faster and most writers remember more because you start to hear the person's voice, inflection, and repeated words he or she used.

When my dad got really drunk once when I was home from college, he told me, slurring, that, "Your mother thinks you don't love her anymore." This wasn't true, but he kept saying it, repeating, "You go out too much. You never see us anymore." That part was true. His voice was low, scratchy, like he had started smoking again. It was the booze.

Make sure, I warn, to keep the script to truth, though. If you weave in that you rescued a unicorn on the way home from school, we will stop believing you, and that damages your **credibility** as a writer, the quality that makes us believe and trust that your story is honest. Ask James Frey, the guy who wrote *A Million Little Pieces*. Once fact-checkers discovered his supposedly true story about kicking drug addiction and serving time was fabricated, the book was publically shunned by bookstores, who let you return the book, and by Oprah, who shamed him for lying on her show, which is the basest form of shaming the general public can imagine.

I encourage you and your class to have a serious discussion about truth in writing. If it isn't already a topic chosen to discuss, it's easy to make it one by questioning the veracity of any narrator from any text you read in a narrative unit. A narrative is, after all, a form of **memoir**, which means it is predicated on the basis of being honest and truthful. A memoir, usually a book-length narrative, is unique only in its hyper-focus on a very specific subject, like kicking a meth addiction. When readers found out that Frey was not an addict, and had not been in jail or in rehab, many struggling with their own addiction or disease felt let down and angry. That is not what you want out of a solid narrative experience.

The discussion that gets overlooked in narrative is often the most crucial: what are the distinctions, if any, among **fact**, **truth**, **honesty**, and **confession**? These words carry meaning. **Facts** are usually attached to proof, although if it were a fact that I felt betrayed when my college boyfriend cheated on me (true story), do I require proof for you to believe me? I can't produce that. I could scavenge through artifacts and scan a note of apology that he left in one of my boots on my front porch one winter. But unless I determine that you need that proof, or that the artifact supports my narrative arc, I have to build trust with you, the reader, so that by the time I disclose this event, you are willing to believe me. You want **truth**, which is my personal recollection told as accurately as I can, and **honesty**, which is my belief that I am telling you how I felt during the true narrative moments. When we tell all of this, with detail and feeling, you have **confession**. Good for you. You've taken the risks to get here.

This brings me to my dad. In the opening, I confessed that my father is a recovering alcoholic. He is. He went to rehab after the home he shared with my mother was foreclosed upon in upstate New York; he had nowhere else to turn. I was moving to Kansas, newly married, starting a Ph.D. program at the University of Kansas. So he packed up his bags, moved out of the house, went to Minneapolis, and checked himself into rehab. And it stuck. He's been clean for ten years.

What is the point of this? **Confessions**, the barest form of honest disclosure, are only as valuable as their purpose. I can confess my father's addiction history to you, and it's not very difficult, because, as hard as it is watching a family member struggle, this disclosure is my father's to make, not mine.

My narrative is about growing up with a father who was drunk a lot. I have written a handful, at least, of narrative essays about this very focus. My father's drinking is a theme in many of my memories growing up in upstate New York. But I have to be honest: my coping, healing, and dating lives were influenced by my father's drinking, and these are the storylines I have to tell. Often, when we resist narrative, it is because it's vulnerable. We're letting someone see more of ourselves than usual. We're risking reputation.

A narrative cannot focus on anyone or anything but oneself, the writing self. Yes, you can write a damn good narrative about your mother dying; Cheryl Strayed published one, "The Love of My Life," that would become the basis of her first book, *Wild*. But her narrative is not about her mother's life. There is background about who her mother is, so we care that she dies. But the narrative is about Cheryl coping with the loss of her mother, and that is an important difference, a crucial difference.

When I think back to my own childhood, I certainly see my dad drunk and yelling. I also see the night he wanted to watch a rare meteor shower on the front lawn. I was 14. I had just come from a late ballet rehearsal at the studio, and because I was new to pointe shoes, I had to soak my toes. I hobbled with my bucket of hot water to the front lawn, where my father, drunk, had lawn chairs waiting for me, himself, and my mother. We sat out there in the dark, staring at the stars. I don't remember seeing a comet, or a meteor shower, but I do remember the happiness I felt with my entire family on the lawn, together, not fighting.

Your narrative is powerful, complex, and yours. Once you discover what you want to write, and once you take the risks of solid narrative writing techniques, you will be thankful. When you are on a job interview, and someone asks you to tell her about yourself, you will be able to. When you have to address a group at work and give some background because you're new to the team, you will. When you want to stand up for yourself, you will. Because you will have known the risks taken with owning who you are and sharing that. You will have accepted the risk. You will have taken a seat on the lawn, and among all those look-alike stars, you will or will not have seen the meteor, and written what was true and real.

©Igor Kovalchuk/Shutterstock, Inc.

SUGGESTED MATERIALS

Edwards, John. "Prison Man Considers Turkey." *In Brief: Short Takes on the Personal.* Eds. Judith Kitchen and Paula Jones. New York: Norton, 1999. 198–201.

Frey, James. "The Truth Set Me Free." *Big Think.* 20 May 2011. Web.

Link: http://bigthink.com/videos/james-frey-the-truth-set-me-free

McDonald, Jennifer B. "In the Details: The Lifespan of a Fact by John D'Agata and Jim Fingal." *The New York Times.* 20 Feb. 2012. Web.

Link: http://www.nytimes.com/2012/02/26/books/review/the-lifespan-of-a-fact-by-john-dagata-and-jim-fingal.html?pagewanted=all&_r=0

Montaigne, Michel. *Essays of Michel de Montaigne, Complete 1877.* Ed. William Carew Hazlitt. Project Gutenberg. 17 Sept. 2006. Web.

Link: http://www.gutenberg.org/files/3600/3600-h/3600-h.htm

Smith. "A Life to Live, This Side of the Bars." *New York Times: Modern Love.* 25 Mar. 2010. Web.

Link: http://www.nytimes.com/2010/03/28/fashion/28Love.html?pagewanted=all

Strayed, "The Love of My Life." *The Sun Magazine.* 321 (Sept. 2002). Web.

Link: http://thesunmagazine.org/archives/2192

CHAPTER 5

Being Absent:
Student Engagement and Writing Persuasively

At the start of my fall 2013 semester, something terrible happened. It was a Wednesday. I had held my classes, had meetings, emailed my brother-in-law Bert, whose birthday it was. At home, my husband Dan was doing laundry when the phone rang.

The call was from Dan's mother. Through sobbing, I learned that Bert had died suddenly from a heart condition. I got Dan on the line. I got off the phone. I got onto my hands and knees and wept.

The next morning, I went to campus to figure out my schedule because we were flying home to New York and we lived in Kansas. I had classes to teach and this was the beginning of the semester. I didn't have a clue how to do this.

The department helped me by supporting my travel needs. I cancelled a week's worth of classes—telling some in person, the others via email. Dan and I flew home for services and a week of hellish grieving.

This story is and is not unique. It is unique because it's mine and Dan's. It's unique because of some of the eerie details, such as Bert dying on his 40th birthday which was also his daughter's birthday. It is not unique in that we all have people we love who die, and this is often unplanned. And we have responsibilities to tend to when this happens. How the tending happens makes all the difference.

Had my dean asked me to provide documentation, or, worse, not approved my time away, many would have suffered: my students, whom I would not have been able to teach. My husband, whom I would not have been there for. Myself, whom I would not have mended. The experience of disallowing someone to mourn, take time, or be away has harmful ripples in a community.

I have not had an attendance, or absence, policy for my students in about a decade. Bert's death fortified in me a high need to revise the faculty's stances on absences—I use attendance and absence synonymously, though one is positive and the other negative. To **attend** is to show up—positive. To be **absent** is to be missing—negative.

When I attended the State University of New York (SUNY) at Geneseo, there was no absence or attendance policy. In fact, faculty members were reprimanded if one was enforced. This is, unfortunately, rare. Years later, when I returned to Geneseo to teach, I discovered a change: the individual instructor could impose an attendance policy, though the college would still not enforce one or support one. Still, this movement encouraged faculty to impose attendance policies.

At Geneseo, we were encouraged to attend because we went to school there. This sounds dumber than it is. The premise was that if you chose this school, and you chose this class, and were an engaged learner of liberal arts and all that the college had to offer, and were paying to get an education, then you sure as hell would attend your classes. Simply put, if you were not going to classes without a realistic reason, then you were acting privileged, entitled, or disengaged. You may not have been these things, but you were behaving in this way.

I went to class because discussions flowed freely day by day. If, say, I missed a class Friday because I was hung over, the professor was not about to clue me in on what she and the class discussed. This is not, as they say, high school.

©Bryan Pollard/Shutterstock, Inc.

Faculty ask for days off. Things go wrong in faculty members' lives, and we expect to be able to take the time to fix the issue or to heal the wound. Your job is to persuade your professors to meet you, as students, where you are. You, as humans, have earned the inherent right, like us, to heal, mend, and fix when something goes wrong. Your side of this contract is to tell the truth, because truth and trust build effective persuasion. Lying to a professor devalues the exercise altogether. You are working on deception then, not on persuasion, when this happens. Instead, build effective, honest persuasive dialogue because it will help in your professional and personal environments as well.

You expect me to be in class. And I am. I do not show up hung over and let you out early. I do not email you that I am sick and today is a skip day. I do not forget to email you and have you show up to an empty room. This is basic. This is what you expect, as students, from us.

The trouble starts when faculty make fun of your dying grandparents. Yes, this happens, and it shouldn't. I have heard too many times to count that a student had "three grandparents die this semester. Yeah, right." And people laugh. Listen, everyone, it's not funny.

Laughing about loss is not funny. If you, a student, lie about a death in the family, I feel sorry for you. This also tells me that we have an unhealthy working relationship because you cannot ask for time off for some reason, and either you don't value that reason or don't think I will. I operate on believing you. I ask the same of you. If you're honest and proactive, asking for time off doesn't have to be unpleasant. This is where we enter **persuasive rhetoric**, or how to convince others of your cause, side, or problem and solution.

Effective Persuasive Rhetoric

When you are in a situation that gives you the opportunity to defend yourself, say when you have to be absent and have a really good reason, you want to be persuasive, which means being logical and reasonable. Before moving through the list below, you first must identify your audience and know this audience. If your goal is to have an absence excused by a professor with a strict attendance policy, be aware of this policy.

What effective persuasive rhetoric needs to succeed:

1. A central premise: what is being argued (needing to be absent from class).

2. Evidence: proof, such as examples, outside research from credible experts, personal testimony (the reason why you need to be absent).

3. Multiple main points: many arguments to prove your central argument (the reason is causing stress, you have to travel, you need to take care of yourself or others, etc.).

4. An ability to acknowledge the opposition: and then return to your side (you are aware that you will be missing important material but believe that your need to be absent outweighs your need to be in class.).

5. Ability to provide recommendations, or solutions, or conclusions that persuade the opponent to act or believe in what you're saying (what can you do to make up the work? Can you email any work? Can you have a classmate take notes for you? Can you accept the consequence of a lower grade?).

6. Logic. You will present the material we covered and use logic. You want to avoid **logical fallacies**, or language that prohibits reason, language that makes your premise or argument false.

   Words and tactics to avoid:

Always, never	If, then	This is true because it is
Everyone, no one	All, none	Best, worst
Right, wrong	Either, or	Using pity or emotion
Drawing a hasty conclusion	Attacking the opposition	

   Consider free-writing a request to miss class due to a valid reason. What do you say and how do you say it?

Six weeks after Bert died, my grandmother in New Hampshire died. This was less unexpected, but still tragic and difficult. More time off. In a typical semester, when a faculty member has an attendance policy, there is usually a set number of absences a student can have before either getting a letter grade docked from the overall course grade, or, worse, being dropped from the course. All told, I was out for ten working days. If I had been a student who had lost two vital members of my family in one semester, I probably would have had to re-take at least one class, or been dropped from at least one class.

Why would someone be punished for having to handle death in the family?

An attendance policy can be rigid. If this is the case with your course, I encourage you to enact healthy and open communication upfront and throughout the semester between you and your professor. Remember the importance of Chapter 3's issues of composing appropriate messages? This skill could not be more vital here. Explain, accurately and logically, your situation. Be clear, honest, and persuasive.

You may encounter faculty members who are unwilling to make exceptions. Be upfront, be early with any known absence that may occur, and be honest. This will help any faculty member grant you space and time for what is happening in your life.

Some faculty members ask for documentation of an absence. In some work environments, when you are sick and absent, you are absolutely not allowed to disclose your doctor's note with your request for time-off documentation. In fact, were I to hand a doctor's note to my Human Resources office, it's illegal for them to look at it. In this way, we're promoting trust. I do not need a piece of paper to tell me that your grandfather died. Having to be put through printing a loved one's obituary is not a humane experience. Trust makes persuasion work. Consider listening to a speech given by someone you don't trust. Likely, you don't believe the orator, or the message, because of this distrust. The message is lost if trust isn't there.

The most powerful way to document an absence is to explain it in accurate, respectful, and specific language. If you skipped class, okay, fine, tell me. I may not allow work to be made up if you simply skipped a class, but opening up an honest dialogue builds trust. If you are dealing with a crisis, or an abusive situation at home, or depression, or anxiety, or low blood sugar, let your instructor know. And know you should not be punished for these things. You should be supported, helped along, and given resources in the course of your mending.

Having students attend my classes matters. It's a big deal. It keeps classes running. This leads me to the most important section of this chapter for you: **engagement**, or, being involved in your educational experience. The opposite of this, checking out of your education, is being **disengaged**.

Assessing Your Engagement, an Exercise

I want you to tap into how often, as an educated guesser, you are fully engaged in your Composition I course. Circle yes or no to the following classroom behaviors. Be honest.

1. I attend all classes when I am able: Yes or No

2. I text at least once during class: Yes or No

3. I look at my phone at least once during class: Yes or No

4. I stop listening at some point during most classes: Yes or No

5. During group work, I do the least amount of work that is necessary   ~   Yes or No
   to get by:

6. I rarely have the assigned reading done before class: Yes or No

7. I try to scan the assigned reading for that day during class: Yes or No

8. I don't take notes during class: Yes or No

9. I make lists of other things I have to do after class during class: Yes or No

10. I don't ask questions even though I don't understand something in class: Yes or No

11. I am not usually a fully engaged student: Yes or No

12. I often leave the room during class: Yes or No

   Now, count up how many yeses you have.

What are the reasons for your answers? If you're disengaged, what is causing you to check out in Composition I? Consider writing your answers in a few paragraphs to gain clarity.

When I was an undergraduate, there was a real emphasis on the participation portion of a course grade. In this way, I learned how to value class discussions. However, I was shy and rarely participated in class discussions. In one specific English course that I loved, I remember the shock of getting a B. I realized that, despite getting As on all my papers, my shyness dropped my grade to a B because I never said a word in class. I took notes. I listened. But my voice was never heard.

Are you someone whom we hear in class discussion? Usually, I eventually hear almost everyone's voice in class by the end of the semester. Yet, I don't discount you if you are truly listening. Likewise, are you someone who speaks just to hear your voice, or to pontificate at the expense of the discussion? If so, check yourself in this situation. Ask yourself if your comments are adding to the discussion. How and why are you enriching the discussion? And then, remember to let others speak to foster a healthy community of engaged students.

Active listeners interject to show you they are listening. The interjections (*uh-huh, yeah, right, I remember*, etc.) are place cards to let the speaker feel heard. However, this doesn't always mean true listening is happening. How many times have you said, "Uh-huh" as someone rambled on and you were not paying attention? This type of listening is what I identify as text-listening. You're in class, and hearing some of the discussion, and you're also texting your friend about lunch. Why?

A better question is, why are you disengaged from class? In some Composition I classes, you will get lectures presented to you. I encourage you to ask questions when appropriate to try to have discussions about the subject. You'll learn, your peers will thank you, and you will likely get richer material from the instructor this way.

Your engagement in class is tied directly to your sense of self-worth. If you are hiding in class, ask yourself why. Investigate your ability to prepare or your ability to join the conversation. I used to be the student who rehearsed answers. I was the one in the back, planning out what I was going to say when someone else said it better or we moved on because I waited too long. Sound familiar? If so, I suggest writing down your comment, and either saying it, or using it in writing assignments. It's valuable and you do have important things to say.

Also, you are not stupid. If some terrible person told you that you were dumb or a bad writer or can't read fast enough, this is not true. I believe in your work because you are in my class. And because you are in my class, you have to try to believe in that work, too. Or else, what are we doing here?

Triggers for Disengaging from Class Exercise

Engagement can look like listening and taking notes. But here are things I see students sometimes doing to ease discomfort, or to avoid being part of class. Read the list and identify any triggers of your own by checking the boxes that trigger you to disengage:

❐ Texting with the phone under the desk / table.

❐ During group work, not turning your chair toward the group.

❐ Using your phone during group work.

☑ During discussions, rolling your eyes at the guy-who-talks-too-much.

☑ During discussions, making a frustrated face at me when the girl-who-talks-too-much talks too much.

❐ Simply refusing to participate in group work.

❐ Taking notes on your laptop during discussions but, really, you're online.

☑ Whispering to friends about what someone just said in discussion.

❐ Coming in late. I mean really late, like 12:30 when class started at 12:00.

❐ Passing notes (Come on!).

- ❐ Asking people around you for a pencil / pen / piece of paper during in-class writing (Come on, it's a writing class.).
- ❐ Listening to music in class.
- ❐ Answering your phone during class (Don't do this. It makes teachers really mad.).
- ❐ Getting the discussion off topic so we don't have to talk about the reading you did not read.
- ❐ Are any of these familiar? Why are they happening?

Consider turning your answers into a persuasive paper. Can you write about why students should be engaged in their educations? What about how to improve teaching practice to encourage more engagement in students? Or how to give advice to a disengaged student, or to yourself? Try it out.

I understand that we, as humans, check out of long discussions. After 50 minutes in a class, you will definitely need a break. In a 50-minute class, that's fine. But generally, in a 50-minute class, you need a break from what we're doing every 15 minutes. That means we should be doing at least three things in class. Sometimes, we have a really long, really dynamic class discussion that goes on and on. That's fine. But if you find yourself disengaging, start to contribute to the discussion, or ask a follow-up question, or actually write notes to yourself. These things not only keep you engaged, but they enhance your experiences during class.

One way to see engagement is in the reverse. How would you like it if I came in, read from the book, looked up after 50 minutes, and said goodbye? That's not an engaged teacher. You deserve to expect an engaged teacher.

If you are not willing to be engaged in class, you're non-verbally saying that this course doesn't matter, or even you don't matter. You're saying you don't have to be here.

I want you to show up. I value your time here. It's why I don't punish you when you're absent. It's also why I cherish the time we have together as a class.

If you are engaged in class, chances are, you are more engaged elsewhere, from your dinner table to your job to your friends. Being engaged means being present, valuing who you are, and valuing those around you.

Yes, can people in class talk too much or pontificate on a single subject? Sure. It's my job to fix that. Your job is to stay involved, stay respectful, and add thoughtful comments to the discussion. Especially, I would add, when you're paying for it. More to the point, you're worth it.

©Peshkova/Shutterstock, Inc.

SUGGESTED MATERIALS

The Chronicle of Higher Education. "The 2014 National Survey of Student Engagement: A Snapshot." *The Chronicle of Higher Education* 20 Nov. 2014. Web.

Link: http://chronicle.com/article/The-2014-National-Survey-of/150153/

Community College Survey of Student Engagement. "2014 Cohort Findings." *CCSSE.org.* 2014. Web.

Link: http://www.ccsse.org/survey/survey.cfm

National Survey of Student Engagement. "NSSE in the News (2014)." *NSSE.iub.edu* 2014. Web.

Link: http://nsse.iub.edu/news/inthenews.cfm

Nelson, Libby. "The Students Who Get the Most Out of College Wake Up and Go to Class." *Vox* 23 Nov. 2013. Web.

Link: http://www.vox.com/2014/11/23/7271727/college-students-morning-sleep

Wallace, David Foster. "This Is Water: David Foster Wallace 2005 Kenyon College Commencement Speech." *This Is Water: Some Thoughts, Delivered on a Significant Occasion, about Living a Compassionate Life.* New York: Little, Brown and Company. 2009. Print.

Watch the speech here: https://www.youtube.com/watch?v=IYGaXzJGVAQ

*Your institution's attendance or absence policy. Investigate this.

CHAPTER 6

Developing Student-Teacher Relationships and Assessment

I was in graduate school when my boyfriend at the time put a chair through a line of windows on the second floor of our rental house. It got worse from there, and I fled to another house to be safe. This story ends with a restraining order and me moving in with my parents.

During this time, I kept up with my graduate work at the State University of New York (SUNY) at Brockport, a state university on the Erie Canal. I also dyed my hair a dark brown, which covered up all my blonde. I walked into my thesis advisor's office. He was a poetry professor, someone who, the summer before, I house-sat for and trusted deeply. He knew the ex-boyfriend who had just terrorized me.

I tearfully told him the run-down of what happened. He did two important things:

1. He asked me if I was okay, and if I needed a place to live. Being asked if I was okay was so reassuring. I was not okay, and he could see that. He didn't focus on if I had the strength to continue my coursework or my writing. He saw me as a person.

2. He made me laugh. After the initial shock of the story wore off, he leaned in and nodded toward my hair. "So," he said, "you in the witness protection program?"

Exchanges like this one happen on campuses every day—or they should. There is a well-known English professor at the University of Kansas named Mary Klayder. She has a chair that has been made famous in her office because she encourages students to come see her, especially in times of trauma or worry. Her mantra, "It will be fine," is used across campus and on social media. She has helped thousands of students simply by being available and fostering relationships with her students. Students interviewed for *Kansas Alumni* said this about her: "She asks questions, she pays attention to the replies, she tries to understand without judging. She gets it." This is an ideal experience, one you, as a student, also deserve.

©SergeBertasiusPhotography/Shutterstock, Inc.

So, how do you develop trust in your relationship with your English professor beyond explaining absences (covered in Chapter 5)? You start by being yourself and trusting that the professor is doing the same. You engage in class discussions, attend office hours, and speak with your professor before and after class when you can. Take advantage of opportunities on and off campus led by or attended by your professor, like attending a reading he's giving, or meeting a visiting author he's brought to campus. Take time to listen and exchange ideas and your thoughts whenever possible.

One major concern that students have is judgment from their Composition professor. This usually happens when, and if, you are asked to write something that could elicit judgment—not should, but could, such as writing a personal narrative (see Chapter 4 on this) or writing a position paper taking a stance on a political or social issue that may or may not correspond with the professor's own beliefs or values. Say you want to write a position paper on gay marriage and your position is for gay marriage rights in your state. You do the research, you present main arguments, you're logical. What happens if you don't know the position your professor has on this issue, or if the professor is against gay marriage? This is important: the professor's beliefs and values do not matter when it comes to being evaluated on your own writing. Your grade should be solely based on the guidelines for the position paper: taking a position, being logical, having research, being clear, etc. Your position itself is not something to be graded or judged in this academic setting. You have an inherent right to own and have your position. This environment asks you to write the position well. That's the grade basis, no matter the professor's position. This is a hard lesson because we worry. But if your work is being judged, and not graded, bring this issue to the professor, to the dean, or the department chair, or your advisor or counselor. Someone needs to know so this stops.

Generating Real Paper Topics Exercise

An exercise in generating real paper topics, or, how to reveal who you are in a safe, nonjudgmental space.

*In two columns, list issues you care about, and also list **pet peeves**, or things that bother you:*

Issues I Care About: Pet Peeves:

If you could write about one item from each list, what would you choose? Circle those. Without fear of being judged, start thinking about how to craft each paper. Opening yourself to write about each of them starts your path to being honest and trusting in your class.

Being open and yourself gets dismissed in too many Composition classes, where you are asked to essentially open yourself to the professor and hope for the best. Here's the important thing: grades are not the same as judgment. **Grades** are a set of tools that evaluate skill level; **judgment** is a mode of personal evaluation that imposes values on a subject or person, and prevents further exploration. If your grades are not skill-based but based on personal judgments in your classroom, again, remember that someone (the chair of the department, the dean of the division) needs to know about it. This is your education.

For instance, in our local newspaper, the *Lawrence Journal-World*, a reporter interviewed students at the start of the fall semester at the University of Kansas. When William Elliott, a freshman from Topeka, was asked what his concerns were, he said this: "'I'm dreading English class. I'm not very good at English. Prof said if you do everything I ask you might get a C, and half of you will fail.'" This is an example of a grading approach based on the fear of judgment and a presupposition that students in this class will inevitably fail. This represents an opportunity for students to advocate for their education and for themselves despite being fearful. Consider your persuasive approach to this. The grading system already seems lodged in judgment. Logically, how can you find a way to succeed and have a good experience in this class? Consider your resources. Could you speak directly to the professor about the dread the grading policy has produced? Telling an advisor or campus counselor about this grading set-up can help navigate this experience. The English department chair or dean might want to know this is happening, too. Grades are not meant to be fear-inducing. They are meant to gauge progress. You deserve to be yourself and explore in a class. Speaking up can impact change.

Take another example, cited in *The Atlantic* article, "How to Escape the Community College Trap," by Ann Hulbert. At the Borough of Manhattan Community College, students in an algebra class had a professor who talked down to the students, making judgments about how easy the course material was. "The class felt mocked," reported one student, and that student went directly to the professor to let him know that the class felt degraded in his class. And in response to this "assertive self-advocacy" on the part of the student, the professor changed his teaching and the class improved. This is a prime example of how the power in the classroom rests largely on you, the students, especially if students collectivize. It's also a reason to practice logic and persuasive rhetoric to advocate for yourself and for others.

©Rawpixel/Shutterstock, Inc.

Grades are not value judgments. This gets tricky. During a recent semester, I happened to have a good number of students who wrote narratives that were what we call risky—vulnerable, honest, confessional—and focused on issues of crime, parental rights, and abandonment at early ages. These narratives were beautiful. Yet, in a handful of cases, the students' content, which was excellent, was marred by the lack of development, or the need for mechanical clarity (the sentences were run-ons, for example), or the lack of a conclusion.

When I handed back a lot of C and D grades, I saw faces fall. Students cared deeply for their work, and they thought the grades indicated my judgments on their life stories, which was problematic.

Instead of moving ahead with the second unit that day, we had a 50-minute conversation about grades and judgment. The students, because I opened up to them about how I graded their narratives, trusted me enough to tell me that they thought the grades indicated judgment. They did not. I asked the students to tell me how long it took them, on average, to complete their narratives. The average was a half hour.

Writing an entire paper in a half hour is not the best choice. I drew a connection between their missing links (their gaps) in their narratives, to the amount of time spent seeing and dealing with the gaps. This was down to minutes. This helped explain the grades.

Just having this basic conversation developed trust between my students and me. After every subsequent paper, we had a conversation about the grades given, the time and effort spent on the work, and if there was a disconnect. That class turned into a functional community of individuals who trusted the space of the classroom. They changed my teaching by trusting me enough to talk honestly with me.

Self-Assessment about Grades

A **self-assessment** is a tool to gauge your academic performance honestly. Try these steps below when you are about to hand in a paper for a grade. Revisit this when you receive the graded paper back:

How long did this paper take me to write? _____

I expect this grade on this paper: _____

I deserve this grade on this paper: _____

Explain, in a few sentences, your reasoning. When you get the grade back, explain any inconsistencies and address areas to improve.

A basis of student-teacher trust is power. Many students view the professor as grader, thereby giving the power in the classroom to the professor. But I can tell you, from personal classroom experience, you have more power than you think. Without you, there is no classroom, no need for a grading system.

Grades are a construct, a system to equalize the work of many in a semester's time. But they don't define you or what you know. Grades may validate your mastery over a subject or show your skill set, but they are not a clear barometer of your education. You and your experiences in college are much bigger than a scale or set of numbers.

In a climate of **assessment** in education right now—meaning the process of figuring out how well the teacher is teaching, how well you as students are doing with the course material, or how impactful or pragmatic the course material is—assessment in your classroom can be another powerful tool for you to build trust with your instructor.

Assessment Exercise

At key points during the semester (especially mid-semester and end of the semester), try assessing the course, either alone or in groups in class.

Ask yourself the following:

- What have I learned so far in this class?

- How can I apply what I have learned in class to other classes / my job / my life?

- How effective is the teaching methodology in this class?

- How effective are my tactics to write papers / complete projects in this class?

- Am I devoting enough time to assigned work in this class?

- What is missing from this course that I or others would benefit from?

These answers are valuable and also show the development of trust if you are able to be honest—both about your performance and the performance of the professor. The answers are also worth keeping and reflecting upon in your **final portfolio,** a document that asks you to assess your progress, struggles, and achievements in the course of a semester.

Academic institutions are using assessment tools now to make sure students are satisfied, and to modify curriculum and teaching practices—this gives you, the student, responsibility and a sense of power. **Teaching evaluations,** usually handed out at the end of the semester, are an assessment tool to rate and explain the professor's teaching tactics and curriculum filled out by you, the students. A teaching evaluation is an excellent gauge of how healthy a professor-student relationship is, because the documents can be anonymous and as critical or as kind as you want the feedback to be. When handled with responsibility, a functional teaching evaluation honestly assesses the teacher, approaches, material, and classroom dynamic with constructive criticism. Take this exchange seriously, and don't let it be the only time during the semester when you speak up or offer feedback. If a teaching practice is not working, let your professor know, if you can, and also let other people at the institution know. Change doesn't happen in silence.

When I was an undergraduate, we had a new professor who wasn't yet **tenured** (under continuing contract), and many in the class wanted to use the end-of-semester teaching evaluation to "get him fired." I remember that day: he brought in candy to pass as we filled out the evaluation for him. I remember thinking that this was a bribe, and that he didn't trust us. I also remember thinking that, if his teaching was really so poor all semester, we should have said something earlier. We didn't, and he gained tenure shortly after that semester. From this, I learned that it is vital to continually engage with my education and the process of assessing it. This matters a great deal and is largely where students' power rests.

There's another tool, a free online teacher evaluation website: Ratemyprofessors.com. Go there. Use it. Read the feedback and the students' comments. And then consider what it is you are looking for in a teacher. This site allows anyone to write unsolicited comments about a professor. Many of my students use it to select their semester's professors. But many have also noted that the comments proved to be false when they got into a class; teaching is a subjective art, and what works for you might not work for someone else. That's why, when you see the comment that a teacher's "an easy grader," or just "easy," be wary. Easy how? And, ask yourself why easy appeals to you in college. You elected to be here. Why, now, do you want your educational experience, something you are paying for, to be easy?

I still keep in touch with the professor who asked me if I was okay, all those years ago. Going to a professor's office hours can be intimidating—but it's not nor should it be (see why and how you can do this in Chapter 7). Trust starts in the classroom—where you interact, engage with, and contribute to the overall health of the class and its sense of community. That means holding yourself accountable as well as holding your classmates and your professor accountable. All parties deserve to have a healthy, trusting relationship. If you can accomplish this, you have moved from being an **extrinsically motivated student** (based on grades) to an **intrinsically motivated student** (based on worth). Here is where true, long-life learning happens. Expect this of yourself and of your professor. It can change everything.

©Alexey Repka/Shutterstock, Inc.

SUGGESTED MATERIALS

Hulbert, Ann. "How to Escape the Community College Trap." *The Atlantic*. January/February 2014.

Link: http://www.theatlantic.com/magazine/archive/2014/01/how-to-escape-the-community-college-trap/355745/

Lawrence-Journal World. "Polling KU on the 2nd Day of Class." *Lawrence Journal-World* 27 Aug. 2014. A1. Print.

Lazzarino, Chris. "It'll Be Fine." *Kansas Alumni* 4 (2014): 30–36.

Mayfield, Julie and Lindsey Mayfield. "Six Ways to Deal with a Bad Professor." *US News & World Report* 26 June 2012. Web.

Link: http://www.usnews.com/education/blogs/twice-the-college-advice/2012/06/26/6-ways-to-deal-with-a-bad-professor

Meier, Deborah. *In Schools We Trust: Creating Communities of Learning In an Era of Testing and Standardization*. Boston: Beacon Press, 2002. Print.

Wecker, Menachem. "5 Guidelines for College Student-Professor Interactions." *US News & World Report* 17 Sept. 2012. Web.

Link: http://www.usnews.com/education/best-colleges/articles/2012/09/17/5-guidelines-for-college-student-professor-interactions

CHAPTER 7

Talking to Your Professor, Office Hours, and Informative Rhetoric

In a Composition class recently, I presented what I call a Three Spheres narrative (Chapter 12 explains it fully). What this meant was that I disclosed a lot of information about my life when I was a college student. Included in this was the disclosure that I was in an abusive relationship when I was a senior. The students gasped—they were surprised, which is part of the reason I tell them.

After class, I went back to my office. A student came to my office hour. At first, I thought she was there to ask a question about the class. When I turned to face her, I saw she was crying.

I asked her if she wanted to sit down; she did. I closed my door. She asked me, "Did it ever get better?" I knew what she meant right away. She was asking if, after I left my abuser, my life got easier.

"Yes," I told her. "It did."

From the narrative work the students had already done in class, I knew a bit about her own history living through, and successfully exiting, an abusive relationship. But in the hour that we talked, we were able to discuss what it meant to feel loss even though we escaped our abusers. We were also able to talk about her recovery and how she was going to make it through her semester. She left feeling lighter, better, than when she came in, and was fortified with a plan to navigate the rest of her semester.

This experience illuminates why building trust between student and professor is vital to the overall success of the student, especially if your institution doesn't have advisors or counselors on site (and even if it does).

In order to connect one-on-one with students, I hold office hours, and I also hold what I call optional conferences. The optional conferences are meant for students to come into class if they need to, and students can expect to receive individual help or feedback from me. Students generally seek help with anything happening in class (and sometimes outside of class, too) during this time. When available, face-to-face conferences can be a great, neutral time for you to ask questions you haven't yet, and to provide your professor with information about who you are and what your challenges and strengths are. You can inform the professor about your skill sets and areas of possible improvement and gain instruction from the professor in this un-intimidating setting. When I hold optional conferences, the experiences I have with students instruct me and are a litmus test of how the course is going. If, say, students come in needing a lot of help writing their persuasive documents, I need to provide more class instruction in that area. If, say, no one comes in, I have to assess if the students are simply working independently that day, or if the students are afraid to come talk to me. If the latter is the case, we have a problem that needs to be addressed.

When students trickle in during optional conference days, which is typical, they ask all sorts of questions. Some are about class, some are asking for draft feedback. Some want help deciding on a major. Some want help in other, more serious, or more divergent, ways, such as a managing a crisis, or an issue with family or friends, or a failed math test, or another challenge we encounter by being alive. In these ways, the optional conferences can be crucial to the development of student engagement and health. Use this time to engage with the instructor and to ask anything you need to ask.

Student Exercise: What I Need from an Optional Conference

Instructions: *Consider where you are in your Composition I course right now. Are you struggling with material? Are you doing well?*

Use this space to identify areas of concern or celebration to discuss during an optional conference:

How writing assignments are going:

My personal wellness:

Family and friendship stressors:

Other academic subjects / areas:

Future plans:

Overcoming other, outside obstacles:

Current level of mastery of course material:

Planning for the remainder of the semester:

How class is going for you:

These areas can help guide your conversations with your professor, and your professor will not only be able to listen and help, but will likely also be able to provide you with campus resources available to you that you may not have known about yet.

Once, I had only one student arrive for an optional conference. She had been a resistant student, one who would not speak in class and one who criticized the reading material in her writing. I was excited to see her in the room when I got there.

The student claimed she didn't know how to begin the next writing project, so we discussed why the book we were reading for that unit was so challenging for her. From this discussion, it became clear that her living environment was unsafe. The optional conference was not truly about the writing assignment: the optional conference provided an excuse, a space and time, for the student to seek help. I was able to connect her with a counselor on campus, one who helped her more than once. In this example, we see the importance of carving out time to engage with and connect with your professors. Being open to this vulnerable space may change everything.

In perhaps less dire ways, talking to your professor during **office hours**, the time your professors have dedicated to talking with you in their offices, about class and related, and unrelated, material, is also a valid, smart, engaging way to deepen your educational experiences. The times when your professor holds office hours should be listed on your syllabus; if not, ask your professor. If you have questions, ask after class, before class, and during office hours. This is another time in which to engage with your professor and offer more in-depth information about who you are and your progress in the class.

There are myths about either attending or not attending professors' office hours. Some students are scared or intimidated to show up, unannounced, to ask a question or clarify course material. Some don't want to impose, or some are afraid of the feedback one-on-one. I waited until sophomore year to go to anyone's office hours, and I only went because my friend made me. I was excited by the course material in a sociology course and wanted to ask the professor a few questions about my final project. No one else could answer these specific questions. So, at the urging of my friend, I ventured in and he told me to sit down. I asked him my questions, and an hour of discussion went by. I lived. I gained confidence. I came away inspired, less confused, and happy I had connected. He answered my questions and made me feel valuable. I walked away with a final goal in mind for my paper, feeling confident and glad to have gone into his office to chat.

Office Hour Myths

Identify whether you think the following statements are true or not:

1. If I go to a professor's office hours, my grade will improve.	True / False
2. If I go to my professor's office hours, I don't have to attend class.	True / False
3. Going to my professor's office hours is the only way to be remembered in class.	True / False
4. My classmates and friends can answer all my questions so I can avoid going to office hours.	True / False
5. I will get privileged information that other students won't have if I attend office hours.	True / False
6. I will get preferential treatment if I go to office hours.	True / False

Office Hour Truths

1. *False.* Your grade is separate from student engagement evidenced in attending office hours.

2. *False.* Office hours can provide supplemental instruction, but office hours are not substitutes for attending class.

3. *False.* Attending office hours continues the dialogues from class; you will be remembered because you're you.

4. *False.* Your classmates and friends likely don't have all the answers, and may even steer you in the wrong direction. Instead, have one come with you to an office hour discussion.

5. *False.* Professors may resent the experience of office hours being treated as catching-up on instruction if you miss class, and you will not get information that is secret. You may simply learn more about the professor or subject area, but it will not be privileged information kept from others on purpose.

6. *False.* You will not get special treatment if you attend office hours.

Office hours are a safe haven for you as a student. They are resource centers, places to go when you need guidance or quiet, help, or support. Office hours are meant to be a place to exchange ideas, extend class discussions, and get to know you better.

Don't worry if you don't attend office hours. You can stay after class, or talk to the professor before class, or even during discussions. But talk. Emailing your professor can also work, especially if you are taking the class online. If you are enrolled in an online class, do write your professor, and engage in this way. Visit online office hours, where you can chat one-on-one. Join online discussions to provide information about who you are as a student to the professor. In a face-to-face class, there is a bit of distance when emailing instead of having a face-to-face conversation. Talking to your professor builds a relationship. This is what education is about—exchanging ideas and talking through theories, concepts, approaches, and styles. This skill, when applied in educational spaces, will also begin to apply to workplaces, and other areas of your life, and your level of engagement, productivity, and overall fulfillment will increase.

Student Exercise: Attending Office Hours

Use this space to write down any questions you currently want answered about what you are doing in this Composition I course. If it helps, consider these areas:

Current writing assignment:

Revisions:

Class discussions:

In-class writing:

My grade:

My participation:

The reading(s) I don't understand:

Outside readings / further research to consider:

What I need to do next:

Now, try to assess each area listed above. Do you have concerns? Questions? Successes? If so, save these and try to ask your professor during office hours. Try it; see how it goes. If it reduces any anxiety you have, you may also make an appointment with your professor to make sure she's available when you arrive. Bring your list of topics with you to remain focused if that helps, too.

An exchange between you and your professor also encourages **informative rhetoric**, which means you and your professor are exchanging information about one another. In Composition I, an informative paper is one in which you research facts and provide information about the subject by being **unbiased**, or objective. In other words, you keep your opinion to yourself about the subject.

Informative writing is often journalistic, in that it requires research, objectivity, and facts that tell us a deep level of information about what is being reported. Having sound informative rhetorical skills means you can find **credible** (reliable) source material and filter research into meaningful text. You gain an understanding of a subject and educate others about it. This skill directly relates to how you interview for jobs and how you perform at work and in any professional setting. If you are asked for information, it is a skill to be able to provide unbiased, informative reporting about the subject, instead of offering your unsolicited opinion of the subject. Being able to communicate information without bias is a vital skill because it offers clear communication, it enhances your ability to see multiple, varied perspectives of a subject, and it offers growth to know more about a subject.

Alternative Student Writing Assignment: Profile

Writing a **profile** is a common Composition I assignment. A profile is a detailed, in-depth, and objective film or piece of writing about a person, place, event, or concept. Being able to conduct **primary research** (research you collect on your own, such as interviews with the profiled subject and her friends), and **secondary research** (finding credible material about the subject that is already gathered), is a valuable skill. Making a documentary, or film, can work, and so can writing a paper as a profile. The goal is to dig deep.

Primary research is research you collect yourself. If your professor is your profile subject, this means interviewing the professor and reporting important quotations from him, using dialogue you have shared (with permission), and recording observations such as mannerisms, speech patterns, and appearance to bring the individual to life. In this way, your narrative detail and description skill sets return.

Secondary research is research already collected for you by someone else. If your profile subject is your professor, this might include journal articles he has published, articles or news reports he has appeared in, photographs taken of him, and other work he has either written or been included in—reviews, teaching evaluations, class assessments, for example.

For a profile assignment, select a subject you want to know more about and begin to gather information about the subject. One option is to select your professor as the profile subject to get to know him or her. Gather information during office hours and before and after class; this can teach you how to conduct primary and secondary research, and it can teach you to appreciate and understand a subject at deeper, more meaningful levels.

Use primary and secondary research in your profile: it enriches the subject matter and affords you the opportunity to make important choices about the most meaningful details of the subject.

Informative rhetoric, in a profile paper, or during office hours, or during a conversation with your professor, is a powerful tool. Your professor wants to know who you are, as a person, and getting to know your professor enhances your education. Informing others about various subjects encourages growth in critical thinking and in your ability to be an effective communicator, which is valued among all professions. Embracing who you are, and what you know, and successfully informing others about all this, is empowering.

When my student came to chat about recovering from her abusive relationship, she successfully informed me of her maturity and coping mechanisms. She informed me that she was self-aware and an advocate for her safety, and that she also knew she needed help to heal. What she also did was inform me that she would be okay, great even, because she came to my office hour, engaged in a vulnerable dialogue, and left with a well-earned understanding of how strong she was, and surely, still is.

©KreativKolors/Shutterstock, Inc.

SUGGESTED MATERIALS

Gordon, Claire. "What Role Does College Partying Play in Sexual Assault?" *Al Jazeera America.* Web. 29 Oct. 2012. [Example of unbiased, profile-based informative writing]

    Link: http://america.aljazeera.com/watch/shows/america-tonight/america-tonight-blog/2013/10/29/what-role-does-collegepartyingplayissexualassault.html

Hartman, Steve. "Everyone in the World Has a Story." CBS News. *CBSnews.com* 11 Jan. 2011. Web.

    Link: http://www.cbsnews.com/news/everyone-in-the-world-has-a-story/

Reitman, Janet. "Confessions of an Ivy League Frat Boy: Inside Dartmouth's Hazing Abuses." *Rolling Stone Magazine* Web. 28 Mar. 2012. [Example of unbiased, profile-based informative writing]

    Link: http://www.rollingstone.com/culture/news/confessions-of-an-ivy-league-frat-boy-inside-dartmouths-hazing-abuses-20120328

Straumsheim, Carl. "Don't Email Me." *Inside Higher Education.* 27 Aug. 2014. Web.

   Link: https://www.insidehighered.com/news/2014/08/27/sake-student-faculty-interaction-professor-bans-student-email

Vanity Fair. "Proust Questionnaire." *Vanity Fair* Various interviews. Web.

   Link: http://www.vanityfair.com/archive/proust-questionnaire

CHAPTER 8

Working in Groups: Class Discussions, Community Development, and Synthesis

During a recent semester, as I was starting class, a student in the front handed me his phone. On it was a text alert that our campus was on lockdown due to suspicion of an active shooter on campus, specifically near or in the building where we were. Our class got quiet. One student wanted to leave and "find" the shooter. I prohibited him from doing that. Instead, we pulled up the local news station's coverage of the event as it was unfolding, and watched it together on the pull-down screen at the front of the class. This was hour one.

As the second hour of being locked together approached, students started interacting: a few started studying for an exam together. A few more shared a phone charger. One student expressed concern and said that he was scared. His parents lived in another country, and he was unable to get ahold of his mother. A female student heard him and moved to his table to ask if there was anything she could do; she then started talking to him, and the students around him. Eventually, they were laughing together as we waited.

It occurred to me that many students get rides to campus (at a community college, I myself take the bus, and many students use public transportation or ride-shares with others). As we learned that all vehicles trying to enter the campus grounds were prohibited from doing so, this became an obstacle. My students did an amazing thing then: they formulated who would drive whom home.

I asked everyone to say, one by one, if they had a car parked on campus to get home with or not, and if they needed a ride, where they were going. When we got to a student who said, "I got dropped off and I live in Lenexa," another student would raise her hand and offer the student a ride home. It was remarkable. These students had only known each other for a few weeks, but in those weeks, they had done group work together, they had spoken to each other, and they had listened to one another during class discussions. In a tense time of actual fear, they supported each other without being asked.

At a community college (and, really, any college or university), we see diverse populations; the average age of a student at the community college where I teach is 27. If you are 18 and new to college, this can be unsettling because people in the room have more life lived (literally, maybe not figuratively) than you. That's okay. In a classroom of acceptance and tolerance, students teach each other what they know. The group dynamic in a class always matters. Why I think group dynamics are important is because a class can (should) become a community and can have the power to transform lives.

I had a very bright student one semester who wanted to voice all his opinions. He was smart and made great connections. However, when other students in the class wanted to disagree with this person, he became combative. Once, he stood up aggressively on a piece of furniture to give an impromptu speech about his side of a political issue. That was not okay. I had to pull him out of class and ask him what was going on; he was very angry. I remember how jarring the experience was for everyone else in the room. Coming back from that was difficult. The student apologized to the class (on his own accord) and we moved forward. But the dynamic of that class was changed, and that was not entirely fair or productive.

Have you ever been in a class where one person monopolizes the conversation? You are sitting peacefully in your chair, and there it is: the same person's hand in the air, the same person is pontificating on a subject you've already covered? It happens and this experience can be very frustrating. You're paying for this experience, after all. So, how do you deal with this?

Many students in a Composition class expect to write and read on their own, as in, they hope a writing class does not expect group work. Yet, if you have ever had a job, or will have a job, or ever be near people, you will work in a group. It's inevitable; from meetings to projects to collaboration in general, you will work with other people. If you cannot do this well, you will isolate yourself and miss opportunities. Working well with others is a skill.

A successful class discussion, something you should rely on and expect in your Composition course, operates like a functional system. Everyone who wants to is able to speak. No one is interrupted. One comment links to the next, the conversation is lucid, flows, and is connective. Respect is given to all sides, all people, in the room. When a student references another's comment, the student's name is used, as in, "What Sharon said about college parties relates to this because . . ." and, if there was assigned reading, this should also be brought up. Trust me, this sounds idealistic but it happens. And it should.

©Botond Horvath/Shutterstock, Inc.

When you read assigned readings (do this, for the sake of your education), mark passages that you want to talk about. This not only advances your ability to **synthesize** (to connect) your ideas with the text, but it also illustrates to the professor and to the other students in class your capability to connect material. This is one of the key pieces of this course: connection.

Connecting—one author's work to another's, your work to another's, you to another person, etc.— makes the classroom and the experiences within it fulfilling. Connection means engagement, and it also means you are not alone, in person and in idea. When you see how your interests, for example, have been studied and researched by scientists in a **journal article** (a published academic written work, reviewed by experts in the field) this not only validates your thinking but also signifies that you have a place in that field of research. Connecting to those in class means not alienating yourself, and it means that you grow.

A key to critical thinking is synthesis work. Let's start with **critical thinking**, the exercise in having thoughts, and elevating these through the process of reading, writing, and connecting your ideas with others' ideas. In Composition, this means you will connect perspectives, approaches, and people's work in meaningful ways. A **synthesis** is a work that combines, and connects, ideas with material from many sources. One way to synthesize is finding commonalities among the work you're reading and stating why these similarities matter. Another way is to find what makes each source distinct from the rest; these distinctions point out gaps and also multiple ways of seeing the same subject.

Synthesis Paper Possibilities

- **A group synthesis**: each group member contributes material about a chosen subject. Your goal is to connect the group members' ideas by thinking critically about their similarities and differences, and what these mean. Write down what similarities the group members have, and also what distinguishes each member's opinion and knowledge about the topic.

- **A persuasive synthesis**: you select a topic or an issue, and conduct research about this topic. Find out what others say and think about this issue. Then, report the many perspectives and opinions about this topic, offering your own conclusions and opinions among the others to argue for or against.

- **An informative synthesis**: you select a subject or an issue, and conduct research about this topic. Report the multiple perspectives and relevant research on this topic without offering your own perspective. State your findings to teach readers the most important points, and the various points of view on this topic.

A way to start thinking about synthesis is to work in groups during the semester. By doing so, you will get to know your classmates and, likely, yourself, better, and be able to navigate differences of opinion respectfully.

To begin to get to know your classmates better, try evaluating where you sit. Usually, students pick a seat and stay there the entire semester. Why don't we move? Because moving means we have to talk to more people we don't know. So what? This is a vulnerable exercise, yes, and it can be riddled with social anxiety. But all you have to do is sit somewhere new. No one said you have to talk to anyone. You can, but start small. From what I've seen, it's likely someone will start talking to you. Classes can be transformative when they become places of exchange and transaction. A class is a great place to practice transactional relationships, where all parties are required to listen, speak up, and form conclusions about what's being said. It is not a time to prove you're always right. It's a time to realize there are other people in the world who have different ideas and opinions than you. Don't change who you are, and don't ask others to, either. Instead, in the transactions of a class, hold everyone (including yourself) accountable to be good, kind humans.

During actual group exercises, where you are put into a mandatory group in class, try talking. I usually see at least one member of a group on his phone, or physically turned away from the rest of the group members. This is a waste of that student's time, and it doesn't help the group out. Instead, try adding what you can to the group, even if that means you simply start by turning to face your group members.

Group Synthesis Exercise in Class

To start: *In your group, select a current issue or topic in the news to research.*

1. First, write down what each group member already knows about this topic.

   Already known: _____

2. Now, if possible, with phones or classroom technology, do some preliminary research about this topic. Try finding **credible research** (research from an accepted expert in this area), and report the information to the group.

   On paper, list each piece of information on this subject that group members found, and include who each source is.

   Source: _____   **Information:** _____

3. Now, explain the information. What does all the information so far have in common, from your group members and from your research?

   Commonalities: _____

4. In a new paragraph, what information is distinct from the rest?

   Distinctions: _____

5. What is still unknown about your topic?

   Need to know: _____

6. So far, what conclusions can you make about your topic? Why is your topic important?

   Conclusions: _____

Whatever you have written so far is the basis of a synthesis paper. If you can accomplish this in class, you can advance this to drafting a Composition paper by extending the connections and elaborating on their importance. Do some research about what's still unknown, and make some meaningful conclusions about the topic, its validity, and who will be impacted by reading your synthesis.

The beauty of working with students in class is that you grow, because you hear and handle various opinions that challenge your own, and you advance in being able to communicate yours. And you will be able to handle class discussions that go south easier, because you know one another and can respectfully set the tone and redirect conversations back into productive space. Conversations will meander—it's part of your experience here. That's okay, because you'll develop the skill of being a patient listener.

Every semester, I have students in class who, for whatever reason, do not get along or like one another. This doesn't mean I foster or endorse toxic situations; I do not. However, strong personalities tend to create strong reactions. This is an excellent opportunity to find where your comfort level is with speaking up, joining difficult conversations, and listening. When you work with people who are different from you in class, you gain perspective about issues related to the qualities your classmates possess, such as age, race, ethnicity, languages spoken, gender identification, sexual orientation, class, and academic ability. In one classroom, you will have an unspoken range of dynamic differences that present a wealth of human perspective and experience. Embrace this, encourage discussion, and listen without judgment.

In most classes, you will encounter someone who talks too much or is not aware that their comments are unrelated to the discussion, or even potentially offensive. A majority of the responsibility to reroute the discussion or have more people involved in the discussion is the professor's. If this is not being mediated, say something to the professor. And, if and when possible, add your comments to the conversation. Say what it is you want to say. Be respectful, which means do not make fun of or attack anyone else, but stand up for your ideas and for rerouting the conversation. I have witnessed excellent communicators say things like, "I am not sure that's in the book," or "The reading doesn't really say that, but it does say this, which relates . . ." or "I can understand where you are coming from, but can we go back to . . ." When you take back the conversation, you are fully engaged in your education, and it's likely that your classmates appreciate the focused effort to get back on track.

A major issue in classes that incorporate a lot of discussion is **stereotyping**, or making assumptions about people in the class. This leads to misinformed judgment, which leads to conflict that is usually not productive. Logical fallacies (covered in Chapter 5) get in our way. For example, stating that lesbianism is "gross" is judgmental, an attack, and intolerant. Saying "all" women are emotional is an erroneous stereotype. You don't like to be stereotyped as a college student, I bet. All college students, for example, are not always hung over. All college students do not procrastinate. Not all college students take out student loans. Just as you cannot use yourself as an example for the entire college campus population, you cannot judge or stereotype your classmates either. In fact, as Isis Artze-Vega notes in her article, "Thriving in Academe," "Many students—notably first-generation college students, and those from underrepresented and low socioeconomic backgrounds—arrive in our institutions with a great deal of anxiety about whether they belong or will be able to succeed". This means that many in the room are experiencing all kinds of levels of hardship or challenge—maybe including you. You are not alone, and you are in a position to be kind to one another in this educational experience. Being in class can be challenging. But at its best, this class is a community and your college experience is your ultimate synthesis.

In one class I taught, I had two men who stereotyped each other and this could have been a disaster. One stereotyped his classmate as a "typical frat guy," meaning he thought he was wealthy, had a chip on his shoulder, and was privileged. The other thought his classmate was "ghetto," meaning he was poor, underprivileged, and possibly dangerous. When we talked in class about issues of college culture, paying tuition, and access to education, they got into conflicts that had to be resolved by me. One student, during a midterm assessment of the course, noted that because of this situation, he felt unsafe to speak up. This was unacceptable and I had to find a way to change it.

I had the students work in groups. I had these two men work together. I did not mediate the group work, but I watched as they had to grapple with current research about college student populations and student loan debt. They began to disclose certain information about themselves, like past hardships, and they explained why they enrolled at a community college. Once they began listening to one another, and were willing to be open to this experience, they began to erase their stereotypes. It turned out that they had similar opinions about politics and about education. Eventually, they became friendly with each other.

This experience helped reshape the entire class dynamic and returned the power to the entire class instead of to only these two men. They also learned a valuable lesson in listening and working through stereotypes. Their synthesis work on education and tuition reform was not only critically thought through and developed, it was connective and lucid—a total success.

One piece of research that I have students look at is the *Chronicle of Higher Education*'s profile of college freshmen at four-year colleges. In it, the reports note some important pieces of student characteristics, which helps urge you not to stereotype when you walk into a classroom. For instance, at a four-year college, 68.3% of students identify as white/Caucasian. 75.8% went to public school prior to college. 72.1% of students identify that they are in the top ten percent, or above average, in academic ability; this might contribute perhaps to how class discussions go, if your classmates believe their aptitude is this high. 86.3% of students decided to go to college to be able to get a better job. That's a large percentage and may dictate how student behavior correlates with grades. So often, students correlate behavior to grades, and forget to absorb the experiences of the classroom on their own. The highest two probable majors chosen were biological science and business. If you're in an English Composition course, this might indicate what your classmates want to talk and write about. These are statistics, so they do not pin down everything about your fellow classmates. But they are helpful in gauging where your stereotypes may be, and how to put them to rest.

Back to the lockdown. After two hours together, my students started to get loud—the good news was they were talking to each other. The bad news was we couldn't hear the hallway messages from the loudspeakers. Finally, I said, "Guys, I think we have to be quiet. Especially because we don't want anyone to know there are people in here." I didn't mean to scare anyone, but that thought was on my mind. Everyone got quiet. Some pulled out their phones and began texting loved ones. Then, someone looked out the peephole: darkness. The peephole was reversed. So, choosing to decide that we were safe, we went back to quiet whispering to reassure each other that we were going to be okay.

Finally, the evacuations began. We were scared, and tired, and hopeful that the shooter was either a rumor or in custody—we didn't know anything yet except the all-clear was issued. Suddenly, an armed police officer barged in, causing most of us to gasp. We were escorted out, and the students insisted on walking each student who was alone to his or her car. Only when all individual student drivers were safe did the groups drive home together; two students headed to Lawrence drove me home that day. This was definitive community spirit in a classroom.

And the community spirit lasted all semester, through disagreements over abortion rights, and politics, through peer reviewing and difficult discussions about hazing and gender on college campuses. These difficult conversations were richer because the students trusted each other, and they knew they would not be judged for their ideas or thoughts. In this way, this class proved that getting to know more about each other in class is what works.

At the end of the semester, the lockdown came up again; we rehashed our ceiling escape plan, we remembered memorable lines from students trying for levity, we recollected the police officer who scared us so badly. It was akin to a family saying goodbye. We had transcended the student who talked too much, or the student who stood on a chair to pronounce his views. Because the students felt safe, and un-judged, they had bonded and had expressed real ideas, opinions, and feelings with grace, candor, and freedom, no speeches needed. And that made all the difference.

©ILYA AKINSHIN/Shutterstock, Inc.

SUGGESTED MATERIALS

The Almanac of Higher Education. "A Profile of Freshmen at 4-Year Colleges, Fall 2012." *The Chronicle of Higher Education online* 2012 Web.

   Link: http://chronicle.com/article/A-Profile-of-Freshmen-at/140387/

Artze-Vega, Isis. "Thriving in Academe: Reflections on Helping Students Learn." *NEA Higher Education Advocate* 33.1 (Jan. 2015): 6–9.

Cain, Susan. "An Introvert Steps Out." *New York Times online* 27 Apr. 2012 Web

   Link: http://www.nytimes.com/2012/04/29/books/review/how-the-author-of-quiet-delivered-a-rousing-speech.html?pagewanted=all

Dweck, Carol. *Mindset: The new Psychology of Success.* New York: Ballantine, 2008.

Hefferman, Margaret. "Dare to Disagree: Ted Talk." *Ted Talks* 2014.

Link: https://video.search.yahoo.com/yhs/search;_ylt=A86.J7s.D8BU0AIALLslnIlQ;_ylu=X 3oDMTB0c2puYm1xBHNlYwNzYwRjb2xvA2dxMQR2dGlkA1lIUzAwM18x?p=dare+to+ disagree+ted+talk&hspart=mozilla&hsimp=yhs-001

Miller, Sarah. "Could You Go 40 Days Without Being Mean?" *New York Magazine* Web. 9 Jan. 2015. *NYMag.com.*

Link: http://nymag.com/thecut/2015/01/could-you-go-40-days-without-being-mean.html

ReducingStereotypeThreat.org. Website.

Link: http://reducingstereotypethreat.org/

Mid-Book Assessment

Please answer all questions honestly to assess and evaluate this book.

Your feedback is valuable and contributes to your overall engagement and success in your education.

Instructions: Circle the word that most accurately answers each question.

1. **So far, this book is engaging me.**

    Not at all   Somewhat   Sure, it's okay   Absolutely

2. **The book chapters are relevant to my life.**

    Not at all   Somewhat   Sure, they're okay   Absolutely

3. **I am learning about ways to write that appeal to me.**

    Not at all   Somewhat   Sure, okay   Absolutely

4. **I think that the book covers material that is important to college students.**

    Not at all   Somewhat   Sure, it's okay   Absolutely

5. **I think that this book is relevant to Composition I students.**

    Not at all   Somewhat   Sure, it's okay   Absolutely

6. **I believe this book is going to get me a job when I finish it.**

    Not at all   Somewhat   Sure, okay   Absolutely

7. **This book will help anyone who wants to be a writer.**

    Not at all   Somewhat   Sure, okay   Absolutely

8. **Writing is an important skill to have today.**

    Not at all   Somewhat   Sure, it's okay   Absolutely

9. **This book's exercises are useful to me.**

    Not at all   Somewhat   Sure, they're okay   Absolutely

10. **I think this book has helpful resources.**

    Not at all   Somewhat   Sure, they're okay   Absolutely

11. **I would recommend this book to other students, writers, or people I like.**

    Not at all   Somewhat   Sure, it's okay   Absolutely

CHAPTER 9

Doing the Work: Drafting, Editing, and Revising

At the end of almost every semester, my students point out to me that we did very little, or no, peer editing. I have nothing against **peer review**, or **peer editing**, which means having other classmates read and comment on your drafts, and offer suggestions for improvement. Students like and dislike this process; it makes students vulnerable because someone else is reading their work, and because the point is to find areas of improvement. This can be difficult if you believe your paper is finished, or brilliant. And it might be both these things, but no paper is ever perfect. Sometimes I resist peer editing because I want students to be in charge of their own work; sometimes classes blow off peer editing days or don't know how to offer helpful feedback. Showing your work to others, though, is always useful. It not only lets someone else see your text with new eyes, it allows you to accept and reject suggestions: you get to filter what needs to be changed and what doesn't. At the very least, make sure you give your papers to someone you trust or believe is a credible reader to offer in-depth, helpful feedback about your work.

Every semester, I have at least one student, usually at least a handful, who somewhere along the line was told that they sucked at writing. Seriously, this happens: a fourth grade teacher criticizing someone's spelling, or a middle school teacher commenting that someone reads too slowly, a high school teacher asking for standards to be met without the creative impulse in the writing someone has done; these are all examples of students' experiences with writing. One of the most important pieces of being a writer is to live in a space of enough confidence to try. Some students are so scared of being judged or criticized that they stick to "safe" subjects and material to avoid being torn down again. Your college Composition professor's job is certainly not to tear you down; it's to make you a well-rounded, adept, and confident writer in many areas of your life. Assessing your writing fears, or your writing over-confidences, is necessary to start really delving into the work you can and should be doing in this course.

©ouh_desire/Shutterstock, Inc.

Student Self-Assessment: Who Am I As A Writer?

Answer each question honestly, and reflect upon your answers at the end.

1. True or False: When I write a draft, I am sure it's done without needing much, if any, revision.

2. True or False: When I write a draft, I am sure it's terrible and I throw it away or don't use it.

3. True or False: I never want classmates to read my writing because I am afraid of being judged.

4. True or False: I wish more classmates could read my brilliant writing.

5. True or False: I usually have trouble starting a paper.

6. True or False: I usually have trouble ending a paper.

7. True or False: I have had an educator or adult tell me I wasn't a good writer.

8. True or False: I believe I am good at writing.

9. True or False: I hate writing.

10. True or False: I love writing.

Reflection

Look back at each answer and consider what each answer means about how you approach writing and this course. If you feel under-confident, how can we build your belief that you have worthwhile things to say and write about? If you feel over-confident, how can we help you address that the writing is never finished, and you can always improve?

Discussion of your answers: *Consider these follow-ups for your answers to the questions.*

1. All drafts need revision. A suggestion: once a draft is finished, put it away for as long as you can. Go back to it later, and read it aloud for changes to be made, both mechanically and in content.

2. Your draft is not terrible. It is common for writers to draft a document over and over. Writers often reveal how many drafts their work has gone through. I have heard anywhere from 10 to over 100 drafts per written document; revising yours once or twice is normal.

3. Feeling vulnerable when someone else reads our work is real and valid, especially when the subject is close to you or about you. Know that most writers feel this way, and that most writers know that their work will eventually be seen by others—it's the point of the work. It's okay.

4. You might be brilliant, and you might not be. That's not for me to judge. But this is a good time to remind you that others in the class are great writers too, and you learn from reading their work.

5. Starting a paper can be daunting. Talk through it with someone, or a Writing Center tutor, or your professor for help.

6. Concluding a paper can also be tricky. Have you written everything that needs to be written? Are you intentionally leaving anything out? Once you have exhausted your ideas, your paper is finished. You can end with something to think about, you can return to the start, or end on a scene. Know that once your writing signals the end, the reader will accept this as the conclusion.

7. I am sorry that someone told you that you were not a good writer. Everyone has a writing strength and you have one. You will find it as you keep writing.

8. You are good at writing. Keep going.

9. Even if you hate writing, you can be good at it and get something out of this class. Select topics that you care about and subjects that interest you.

10. I love writing, too. Good for you.

Drafting work can be tedious because students, and writers, grow weary of their own writing. But, to be a great writer, one has to be a great drafter. **Drafting** means to write what you can, and to craft as much of a first copy of a paper as possible. To begin, consider **brainstorming** your topic and what you want to write about it. This means making an outline, or a list, or some notes, about what your paper will include. Then write it all down. After writing it all down, take another look, or read the paper aloud, and have someone else read it as well. What needs to be changed? **Revising** happens next, which means to change the content of the paper. To revise means to add, subtract, or alter the content of the writing. Be warned: when you alter any content, you impact the content remaining in the text.

©violetkaipa/Shutterstock, Inc.

Once, in college, I had an English professor who taught me a valuable lesson. He asked me what my favorite line in some writing was that I had done, the one line I knew was great in my document. I identified the line, pointed to it. "Take it out," he said. He was sort of an intimidating man, so I started getting nervous. "You're writing toward this line and away from this line. This line is weakening everything else in here." I did take the beloved line out, and he was right. Once I started elevating all my writing to the standard of that one line, my writing improved, and so did my confidence. You can have a paper full of good lines, not just one lonely, cherished, sad line.

Once you have revised your document, **edit** it. Editing means to go line by line, looking for mechanical and grammatical errors, finding places where you repeat your point, places where your citation style isn't right. Editing is the last step to making the document polished and easy to read.

My students do all these steps for each paper. Once, I had a student who was somewhat tentative about starting a synthesis paper in one of my Composition classes. Returning to college after time in the military, he was nervous his writing skills had atrophied (they hadn't). He also didn't know quite where to start. The assignment was to write a synthesis paper about a topic of interest, using research from various credible sources to discuss all the possible perspectives of the chosen subject.

What follows is that student's original draft: you can see it is his own brainstorming technique. This small step led to an extraordinarily powerful paper, which you'll see next.

First, study the brainstorming the student did:

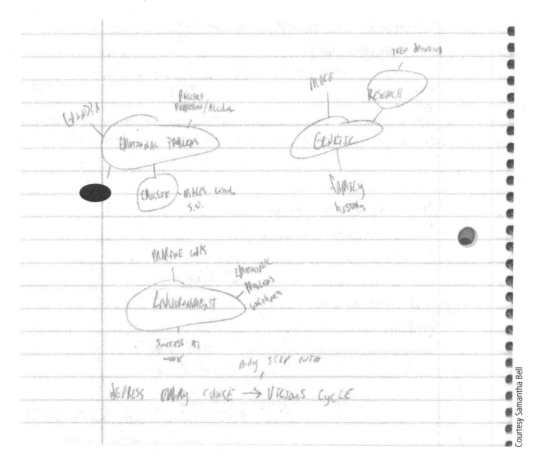

Courtesy Samantha Bell

Does this make you feel better about starting a paper? It should. Each bubble represents one of the student's main points that he wanted to investigate about the subject of alcoholism and its possible causes. The tendrils are points he wanted to add—guide posts, almost, for what to write about.

Here's his finished paper. On the right, write your responses to the questions as we go.

The "Why?"

Alcoholism has been classified as a mental illness, or a disease. At times this has caused some heavy debate. Addiction specialist Dr. Phil Stringer asks, "How many people who never decide to drink would 'catch' the 'disease' of alcoholism?" He goes on to say that "the disease theory" does nothing but allow the person a way to avoid taking responsibility for their actions ("Disease"). However, recovery specialists argue using the analogy of waking up with a song stuck in your head. You may try whistling, or singing another song, but no matter what, that silly little tune just keeps playing all day. It's a simple example of mental obsession, but it's a thought process you have no control over. They believe this is the nature in which alcoholism is a disease (Buddy). Recovery counselor James West, M.D. says studies show that when treated as a disease alcoholism has a 80%–90% success rate vs. when treated as a lack of self-discipline that number drops closer to 30%. He claims "Alcoholism has a large genetic component just like diabetes; you can't talk someone out of being an alcoholic any more than you can talk a diabetic out of being a diabetic" (West). I stand by the belief that the classification of alcoholism is irrelevant. Research proves that when treated as a disease, individuals

---

Is his introduction engaging?

Meh, not really

If not, make a suggestion for improvement:

It could start with action, like a scene. Or, more simply, it could start with the question

What is his paper's focus (thesis)?

The classification of alcoholism is irrelevant

that suffer from it are much more likely to recover. If classifying it as a disease is what it takes to help those in need, then that's what it is.

"Mendacity is a system that we live in, liquor is one way out and death's the other," said American play writer Thomas Lanier Williams III, better known by the nickname Tennessee Williams, in regards to his drinking. For me this quote perfectly describes my thought process, the ability to, if only for a few short hours, escape reality. There are many different factors that may lead an individual to an increased chance of alcoholism: the way they are raised, the environment they are in, problems they may encounter during life, as well as a genetic predisposition that may occur. My problems with alcohol have been something that I reflect upon often. I want to make sense of it all; I want to know why.

Exactly why alcoholism runs in families is not entirely known. Is it simply a learned behavior? Is there an inherited "alcoholic" gene that is passed on? Is it because of certain personality traits that may be inherited, such as having an obsessive or addictive personality? There is plenty of research that can support many different theories, and people may not agree on the why, but the fact remains alcoholism runs in families. When I look into my own family history I can see a possible genetic predisposition that may have put me at an increased risk. On my father's side, there was my great-grandfather. Even though I only met him a few times as a very young kid before his death, I have heard many stories. My grand-

Is entering his own narrative into this paper effective?

It makes him have more ethos on the subject, but it would have been more effective to tell his experience as a story instead of just saying that he was an alcoholic

father's mother died of leukemia when she was only 25. This crushed my great-grandfather and sent him into an episode of depression that he was never able to escape. I don't know his whole story; I don't know if there were several other things that played in, but I do know he turned to alcohol. His alcoholism caused so many problems that by the age of four my grandfather and his brother were taken out of his custody and adopted by their grandparents. My dad claims "It's a sad story really; alcohol just controlled all facets of his life."

My grandfather's brother David, who was removed from the house as well, encountered his own problems with alcohol throughout life. He was in and out of rehabs, bouncing from state to state, job to job. As I understand it, he never had a problem finding a job because he was a fantastic auto body mechanic. However, he couldn't hold a job more than a couple months before being fired for alcohol related incidents.

On my mother's side there is my grandfather. Neither my mother nor any of her siblings talk very much about their childhood. The few times I have talked to my mother about her childhood you can see the pain in her eyes as she thinks back. My grandfather was not a great role model when it came to being a father. He brought back things from the war that many people will probably never know or understand. He was in and out of rehab more than once, as well as in and out of the house constantly. He wasn't home all too often, and when he was, he was frequently drunk.

Is it okay with you to end this paragraph with a direct quotation?

I feel that it is alright, since it kind of sums up ends the scene

Are his examples helpful?

Eh, would like more elaboration on each if possible

My older cousin on my mother's side has struggled with addiction with both alcohol and drugs throughout his life. He has spent time in rehab, AA meetings, half way houses, and prison. Unfortunately the pattern continues to cycle. Family history is not the only genetic quality that may have come into play. According to studies conducted by Columbia and Yale researchers, men are twice as likely to develop alcoholism as are females. During their studies they discovered that the release of dopamine, the neurotransmitter in our brain responsible for rewarding experiences and pleasure, is released at a much higher rate in males than in females while consuming alcohol. They believe "This may contribute to the initial reinforcing properties of alcohol and the risk for habit formation" ("Why"). Being a male with a family history of alcohol abuse and addiction may have put me at a genetic disadvantage of developing alcohol problems.

Almost all rehab counselors or facilities will testify to the amount of impact an individual's environment can play into alcohol abuse. It's fairly easy to see and understand that I was in an environment that was not healthy for my addiction problem. I enjoyed my time on active duty military. I believe in the Marine Corps, and everything it stands for. However, in my experience the military in general is an environment that may lead to or reinforce alcohol abuse. I have never seen the phrase "work hard, play hard" lived out truer than during my four years of active duty

Respond to his narrative: can you relate? Is it helping the paper move ahead?

I can't relate, but it is good to hear more narrative

military. I cannot speak for every branch, or even the entire Marine Corps, but in my experience a "show no weakness" mentality was constantly implied. I don't mean to suggest whether this is right or wrong, or whether this should be the mentality for a military setting or not. However, there is no doubt in my mind that this behavioral trend has had a direct connection to some of the outrageous military statistics concerning PTSD, domestic violence, suicide, and alcohol abuse.

Another part of my environment that may have led to my struggles with alcohol was simply my success at work. I didn't want to stop; I didn't want to think about my problems. If I worked hard enough and drank long enough maybe they would just go away. This led to a work ethic that was not only praised, but rewarded. My work success became a fool's gold. I didn't need to change my actions because it wasn't negatively affecting my work. As a society I believe we have an image, an image that says alcoholics can't hold a job. Alcoholics are old men. Alcoholics are generally homeless. Alcoholics struggle within their careers. Alcoholics continuously drink in the morning. If we don't fit every aspect of the image, we must not have a problem.

The things we experience during life and the way we handle our problems can lead to alcohol abuse. I didn't do myself any favors when I began drinking after my grandfather's death as a teen. The National Institute on Alcohol Abuse and Alcoholism report studies that "teens who had

Discuss the ways the writer uses research in this.

He mentions statistics only evalitatively

Is his research effective?

Why or why not?

Not really, since we don't see the numbers and they are briefly mentioned

an episode of major depression are twice as likely as those who aren't depressed to start drinking alcohol" and develop drinking problems later on ("Depression Health Center"). When the relationship with my fiancé ended, the way I handled it may not have been a surprise, but it most assuredly enhanced the chance of forming alcohol abuse behaviors. Studies show that after divorce, men experience a higher chance of committing suicide, they are more apt to alcoholism, and increase their chance of developing mental health issues. When a man loses his wife it affects his psyche almost identically to the death of a family member or close friend (Morrison). I am aware that these concepts are referring to marriage but after being together over 5 years I have no doubt that some of the mental connections were somewhat similar to marriage.

According to the non-profit organization Help Guide the second highest trigger for depression in men is marital or relationship problems, and the third highest factor that may make them more vulnerable to depression is drug or alcohol use ("Depression in Men"). The Substance Abuse and Mental Health Services Administration reports when depressed, dispirited, irritated or angry, many men turn to alcohol, "Alcohol abuse is extremely common among people that may be depressed, and it is especially common among young and middle-age males." It is also common for them to throw themselves into their job, with the idea of hiding their depression from themselves, friends, and family ("Men"). After the loss

Can you tell this paper is moving toward a conclusion?

Not yet...

of relationship with my fiancé I had become a statistic. When Michael died 8 months later, still dealing with the mental lingering's of before, my mind knew what to do. The pain of his death and the guilt were heavy. No matter how hard I tried; the guilt of my last words to him, the guilt of not being there, and the guilt of simply being alive wouldn't go away. I did exactly what I had programed myself to do.

So again, I ask why? Why did I turn to alcohol? Why has it controlled me with so much intensity over the last several years of my life? Was it because I was at a genetic disadvantage as a male with a family history of addiction and abuse? Was it because of the environment that I had placed myself in? Was it because of terrible decisions I made when dealing with negative life events? Yes. I may never know what had more influence over the others, or if they were all equal in value. However, I am certain that all three of them were at least somewhat of a contributing factor.

Don't misinterpret, I place responsibility nowhere but on me. All of these factors merely put me at an increased risk, and correlation does not equal causation. I live with the choices I have made, I live with the consequences.

Is the tactic of asking questions working?

Sure

What grade would you assign to this paper?

90%

Explain.

Hard to say, since idk the rubric, but 90 felt about right

Debate this grade as a class.

Works Cited

Buddy T. "Alcoholism as a Disease." *About.com*. About.com, 2014. Web. 26 Mar. 2014.

"Depression Health Center." *WebMD.com*. WebMD LLC, 2005–2014. Web. 26 Mar. 2014.

"Depression in Men." *HelpGuide.org*. HelpGuide.org, 2014. Web. 26 Mar. 2014.

"Disease Concept of Alcoholism- the Myth." *Soberforever.net*. Saint Jude Retreats, 2014. Web. 26 Mar. 2014

"Men and Depression." *MentalHealthScreening.org*. MentalHealth-Screening.org, 2014. Web. 26 Mar. 2014.

Morrison, Kyle. "Men After Divorce: Ego, Self Esteem, & Recovery." *HuffingtonPost.com*. The HuffingtonPost.com Inc., 2014. Web. 26 Mar. 2014.

West, James M.D. "Why is Alcoholism Classified as a Mental Illness?" *BettyFordCenter.org*. Betty Ford Center, 2009-2014. Web. 26 Mar. 2014.

"Why Are Men More Susceptible to Alcoholism? It May be in Their Dopamine." *ScienceDaily.com*. ScienceDaily LLC, 2014. Web. 26 Mar. 2014.

This student's paper received an A. Discuss this grade in class and if you think it's earned. Explain what works in his paper and what doesn't—what are areas to expand upon or omit?

For me, this paper satisfied all the guidelines and demonstrated a mastery of synthesis work: the student presents credible, varied research on the outlooks and perspectives of the causes of alcoholism, he uses personal examples, and he narrates his connection to the subject. And still, we can find areas of improvement: writing is a fluid process.

What comes next is the student describing his writing process for this paper, how he became a writer, and his advice for you.

Student to Student: A Former Student's Approach to and Advice for Writing

1. What were you like as a writer when you arrived in this Composition course?

   When first arriving, I believe I was your fairly typical college freshman. Granted, I had done a little writing while in the service, but most of that was fairly technical and emails.

2. How did you decide on this paper topic?

   This is a fairly tough question to answer. I was at a pretty low point in my life and I had already discovered that for me, writing about problems with my life helped me tremendously to deal with them. To me, the topic came almost naturally. I chose my central theme as, why I struggle with alcohol, because I honestly didn't know. Personally, I believe this is the best way to write a synthesis paper, with a question and unknowing of its exact answer. I began to think about what the different possibilities could be and why each possibility may or may not be correct. The writing basically took care of itself.

3. How did you figure out what to research for this paper?

   I got a bit lucky on this aspect. Research kind of lends itself to many of the topics that I discussed in my paper. I talked with Professor Bell several times, and she helped me figure out which parts of my paper the synthesis and my own opinion were strong enough, and which parts could really benefit with research. The great thing about research is that sometimes you discover something you had never thought of. Or find something you want to research more and add into your paper.

4. How have you changed as a student writer?

   I've become much more comfortable with my writing style and confident in my writing ability. I've discovered that nervousness, that anxiety you get before writing is something that happens to everyone. I've learned to trust myself, the writing process, and my professors' teaching. I've learned that everyone's first draft sucks, and if you're anything like me, so will your 2nd and 3rd draft. I've changed my approach from trying to make it perfect the first time to simply getting something down I can work with. Even the best writers revise, seek others' opinions, and revise more.

5. What advice can you give to new Composition students about writing?

Talk to your Professor! I can't stress this enough. They are honestly there to help you. Almost all of them want nothing more than to see you succeed. To progress as a student. If you asked Professor Bell she would probably tell you she saw me at least three times for each paper she assigned. Outlines, organization, research ideas, and working drafts are all things Professor Bell helped me with throughout the semester.

I would also say start early. Give yourself time to do revisions. The last thing I would suggest is that whenever possible choose a topic, or central focus, that means something to you. I believe writing about something you have a vested interest in makes it easier to put in the time and work necessary to get your paper the way you want it. Have fun with it. You never know, you just might surprise yourself with how well your papers turn out. I know I did.

My former student came into Composition as worried and as ready as you all have been: he was open to writing and to the process of discovery, especially by investigating his own narrative and how research helped him process who he was and what he had endured. He is a unique student, and so are you. Remember that writing is a process, and so is being human. We talk together, we read together, and we write together. This student was one who was resistant to narrative work and writing papers in the beginning; he not only realized his talents, but began to believe in himself. Writing can help us change who we are and how we see the world. I am proud of this student (and so many others) because he believed in the risk and he tried his best. His best, as we see, was outstanding. Aim for this.

At the start of a new semester, this student arrived at my office, beaming, excited to tell me he enrolled in another writing course. This is a moment of his success. And all he had to do was start—pen to paper, finger to keyboard—and begin writing.

©MOSO IMAGE/Shutterstock, Inc.

SUGGESTED MATERIALS

Lamott, Anne. "Shitty First Drafts." *Bird by Bird*. New York: Anchor, 1994. 21–7. Print.

Paris Review Interviews. "Susan Howe, The Art of Poetry No. 97." Interviewer Maureen N. McLane. 2012. Web.

   Link: http://www.theparisreview.org/interviews/6189/the-art-of-poetry-no-97-susan-howe

Purdue Online Writing Lab (OWL). "Talking about Writing." *owl.english.purdue.edu* 2015. Web.

   Link: https://owl.english.purdue.edu/owl/resource/755/1/

Strayed, Cheryl. "Dear Sugar, The Rumpus Advice Column # 48: Write Like a Motherfucker." *The Rumpus.net* 19 Aug. 2010. Web.

   Link: http://therumpus.net/2010/08/dear-sugar-the-rumpus-advice-column-48-write-like-a-motherfucker/

CHAPTER 10

Covering the Bases: MLA Format & Research

When I first started teaching, I was young and didn't know what I was doing. Feel familiar to being a student? Probably.[1] I was supposed to teach students how to write papers in various formats, and I was to teach them how to cite their research. When I was grading their first papers, I read one student's whose voice didn't ring true in the writing. Usually clever and a sarcastic writer, this student's voice was rigid, almost scientific, and a great deal of the wording was technical expertise about the subject—the wording read a great deal like a journal article might. At that time, there was rudimentary software for professors to check for plagiarism (now, with Turnitin.com and others, this software is much more advanced to detect cheating). I plugged in a few of the student's sentences, word for word, and behold: the entire paper. The student had copied and pasted a paper already written, online, and labeled it as his own.

I was astonished. I took it personally. At the next class, I asked the student what happened. His shade of red was awful, a blushing tomato. He said he ran out of time and was very sorry. I gave him an F, told him to speak up next time before doing this, and that, if it happened again, he would fail the class and the plagiarism would be reported to the university. University and college policy, at every institution I am aware of, has an active plagiarism reporting procedure; if you plagiarize once, or twice, this goes on file, and can be reported to transfer institutions, or prohibit moving forward in one's educational career. English professors consider plagiarism a big deal.[2] Do you?

©Dooder/Shutterstock, Inc.

Plagiarism is claiming someone else's work as your own, intentionally. There are grey areas to this. One is the issue with reading. When I read too much of one author, I start, unintentionally, to use their wording, pacing, verb choices. And this can happen with movies, television, video games—anything we consume a lot of can seep into our own lexicon. I was so embarrassed in graduate school when my husband Dan was reading some of my creative work and stopped. He said, "Um, Sam, honey?" I

---

1. Not knowing what you're doing is part of the fun. Seriously. Exploring is good.

2. I used to take grey area plagiarism much more seriously than I do now. Even as I wrote this memory of punishing a student, I was like, *Whoa, Sam, let's all calm down.* The point of the discussion is usually why the student copied and pasted a document that wasn't his own. What went on that he thought this was okay? That is the question worth exploring. Isn't this fun? This is NOT MLA format, which makes it more fun.

looked up. "This," he said, and pointed to a line of text, "this line is directly from *The Wonder Years*." And it was.[3] It was from my favorite show in the 1990s, which was narrated. I stole the man's narrative as my own. Because the issue was brought to my attention, I removed the line. However, it wasn't intentional plagiarism because I didn't mean to lift the line. I thought, truly, that it was mine (and nostalgic, evocative of childhood dusks, and very sweet). Nope. I also thought Fred Savage, the main character of *The Wonder Years*, would marry me one day. Again, no.

A professor at the University of Pennsylvania, Kenneth Goldsmith, is famous for being a poet and an innovative writer, along with teaching a class called "Uncreative Writing." In his work, he posits that no new work is original: every work is derivative of something that went before. The original text does not lie within us any longer. Some writers reject this based on believing that art is new and subjective. Other writers believe this *is* true, and it takes the pressure off the need to be new. Goldsmith's class asks students to craft text that is only other people's writing—he calls this *patchwriting*. The students must find connections and transitions among the separate writings, and organize them into something coherent. Goldsmith writes that, by the end of the term, students have a renewed vigor for writing on their own, and this also helps students see how outside text can and cannot be made meaningful to our own work and ideas. This is the goal: to figure out where and how your writing meets other people's in meaningful ways (synthesis work does this, too).

Exercise: Trying to Patch Together Quotes

- Pick a topic you are interested in, or reading material you find compelling.

- Lift direct quotes (word for word) into a new document. Put as many quotes as you can find into this document.

- Now, rearrange them. Highlight ones that go together, and cut and paste them together for coherence. Do not write any transitions among the quotes.

- Fit all the quotes together in a new document that can be read aloud or by another individual. Share these with your classmates to see if yours, and theirs, make sense.

- To debrief, talk about your process: how did you make decisions to fit the quotes together in a manageable way? What is the focus of your new document, and does the focus come through?

This exercise teaches you a lot about how to fit research into your own writing: it should have a specific, meaningful place in the text to fit, so it doesn't disrupt your writing, and adds meaning to advance the writing instead. If you can do this cut-and-paste patchwork, you can certainly fit research into your own writing.

---

3. The line was something like: "I grew up on a street, like any other street, in a town like any other town." Yeah. I love *The Wonder Years*. This is a sappy show about life. Go, right now, and watch the first episode on Netflix. It will change your life. There's music and a first kiss in the woods. Drop everything to see this.

In Composition I, you will likely be exposed to research, citing, and listing your sources at the end of a paper. This practice is a common one in any English class. We, as humans, like to refer to work from other people, movies, media, reports, journals, etc. because this enhances the discussion and deepens our education. It also gives us more credibility as writers. In English classes, this **citation style**, or the way you name the sources of your research, is called MLA format.[4] **MLA format** is from the Modern Language Association, a group of individuals who agree annually on how each type of research used should be named in your paper, and how the source should be explained at the end, in the form of a list. In this way, when you cite your research, you avoid plagiarism by citing your research (as long as the writing itself is your own).

Research: What's It For and How Can I Use It?

First, determine what your paper topic is. Are you writing a persuasive paper? An informative paper? Once you have your topic, try these steps to identify types of **credible research**, or research that is from an expert in the area being discussed and up-to-date.

1. What is your topic: _____.

2. What do you want to know more about your topic? _____

   _____.

3. What kind of research applies most? Select from this list:

   - A documentary

   - **A peer-reviewed journal article** (This is an article, usually looked up with your campus library online database system, that has been reviewed by other experts in the field and okayed for publication. An **academic database** is like Google for academics; it subscribes to academic journals by subject).

   - A textbook chapter

   - A book chapter

   - An online newspaper article

   - A magazine article

   - A medical website

   - A medical textbook

   - A photograph as evidence

   - A website

---

4. Again, to be clear, this footnoting system is not MLA format. No way.

4. Find information that could support and enhance your topic from this source list. Go to the library, or search through the **library databases online** (subscriptions to academic journals online purchased by your school, searchable by you), or try the Internet, to start looking.

   Use **keywords**, specific words and phrases to get accurate matches with your search, to find useful information. An example: your topic is depression in college students. Try the keywords "depression and college students," or "depression, college students," or "depression, college." The more you research, the more specific wording you will see.

5. Once you find relevant information—information that you can discuss and connect within your own paper, write everything you could use down, email the research to yourself, save it to a flash drive, or print the material.

As you saw in Chapter 9, MLA format is a way to cite all the information you have about a source. **In-text citation** means you cite your sources in the text of your paper to be a credible writer and researcher.[5] There are a few ways to cite your information.

In-Text Citation Styles in MLA Format & Works Cited Page

Here's your research:

Topic: Depression in college students

Source: Online Mayo Clinic Staff

Title of link online: "Depression"

Date it was published online: 2015 (the copyright on the bottom of the page says 1995–2015, so you select the most recent date)

Date you viewed this online article: February 20, 2015

How do you know it's credible: Generally speaking, credible organizations have .org and .edu web addresses. Specifically, we see a link on the Mayo Clinic online website labeled: Meet Our Medical Editors, and it then lists every individual and the credentials of each.

Information you want to use: "Depression is a mood disorder that causes a persistent feeling of sadness and loss of interest."

---

5. Don't use footnotes if your professor is serious about MLA format. Seriously. Some people really care about this. Maybe, if you're lucky, you can play around with other citations styles later—like APA, or Chicago style, or this one.

Ways to cite this in your paper:

1. According to the Mayo Clinic staff online, "Depression is a mood disorder that causes a persistent feeling of sadness and loss of interest."

   You have introduced your source in the sentence, and have a **direct quote** (a word-for-word reproduction of the text from the source in quotation marks).

2. Depression is commonly known as: "a mood disorder that causes a persistent feeling of sadness and loss of interest" (Mayo Clinic Staff).

   You have a direct quote and cite the source in parentheses at the end.

3. Depression is referred to as a condition in which people feel less happy and disengage from life (Mayo Clinic Staff).

   You have **paraphrased** the information, or summarized it in your own language, and cite the source in parentheses.

4. The Mayo Clinic staff understand that depression is a condition that persists.

   You have paraphrased the material and name the source in the sentence.

All styles work in MLA format. If you have a page number where your information appeared, say, if the Mayo Clinic published this entry about depression in a manual, and you see the page number online or get the manual, the options are:

1. According to the Mayo Clinic staff online, on page 8 of their article, "Depression is a mood disorder that causes a persistent feeling of sadness and loss of interest."

2. Depression is commonly known as: "a mood disorder that causes a persistent feeling of sadness and loss of interest" (Mayo Clinic Staff 8).

3. Depression is referred to as a condition in which people feel less happy and disengage from life (Mayo Clinic Staff 8).

4. The Mayo Clinic staff understand that depression is a condition that persists (8).

Once you start practicing this, you'll get the hang of it.

A **Works Cited Page** is a list of your sources that were named in your paper, listed at the very end of your paper. You list them in alphabetical order and can see in Chapter 9 a full example of one. The point is to look up the entries you have (like a journal article, medical online site, etc.) and give all the information you have about the sources in MLA format. Here's what the source above would look like:

Works Cited

Mayo Clinic Staff. "Depression." *mayoclinic.org* 2015. Web. 20 Feb. 2015.

That's it. I recommend, when you have to make your list, using a writing manual (probably listed on your syllabus) or asking your professor, or OWL at Purdue online, or the campus Writing Center, for help).

MLA format is a formula and I don't expect my students to get it perfect, ever. The point is to try so that you can give yourself credit for all the research you did and put into your paper, and to let your reader know more about your topic—and where to get this information.

I have had experiences with my own publications where the editors changed the format to their liking—I tell all my students this, because it means that citation styles are fluid, ever-changing with technology and what a credible source is. Our academic endeavors are changing from simple papers to other realms, like digital work, or art and text, or moving images; MLA formatting is a work in progress for you to try.

When I was in college, I was encouraged to consider that books, textbook chapters, and journal articles from academic databases were credible research. I started to open this up when I was in graduate school to understand what else research can be. Research can be a lot of things, like a film, or a piece of artwork, a video game's text, a text message, a tweet on Twitter, and the list keeps evolving.[6] The point is to match your area of research with your research sources. So, if you are writing about the reasons why video games may cause violent acts in reality, I suggest finding research on actual news articles when a violent act was correlated to video game playing, and I would refer to specific video games and their operations to show what they look like in real life. I might seek out published interviews with game makers, and journal articles in psychology and sociology journals that study this topic (they do, and most posit there is not a correlation, but that's okay, this is your dream). Once you open up the possibilities for what research is, the work not only gets more interesting, but also likely more fun.

When I ask my students at the start of a semester to identify what they know about MLA format, most panic.[7] That's because we were taught to know this formula. I say, it's okay not to know. It's not okay not to try. Citing your sources the best way you know how to is a good start. The rest can be looked up for perfection in the style. There are many other citation styles (APA, Chicago style, etc.) that you might encounter in other classes or professions. These, too, we learn from manuals. That's okay. The point is to give credit to the research that is not yours.

If you like looking things up online, a way to check your citations and your Works Cited Page entries is to go to OWL at Purdue (the Online Writing Lab). They have a tab for most citation styles, and they give examples of almost every possible type of source and how it should be cited. As I write this, I see that you can manage and plug your sources into Microsoft Word for help, and software programs like EasyBib are meant to help as well. Your Writing Center on campus can help, too. The point, in a Composition I class, is to try. This will help when you have papers assigned with research needed—this happens in most classes, even some creative writing ones. The more you practice this, the better and easier it gets—or at least less daunting.

---

6.   You can find ways to make what you love into research, depending on the topic. If say, you really love blogs about cats (who doesn't?), you can, with the assignment options permitting, make your focus about people who blog about cats (and good luck: it's a million and counting). If you love serial killers (honestly, so many students do—why does this happen?), find documentaries about some. The more you consume about a topic, the more you'll find as research.

7.   By comparison, I could not, right this second, come up with the Pythagorean theorem. I first spelled the term with an M, PythagoreaM and called it an equation. I was way off, so I Googled it. I use the Internet, and you can too. There are resources online, like OWL at Purdue, for you to use. Everyone says not to use Wikipedia, but they're trying to make this source a fact-checked place for real information; have a class discussion about this site.

Citation styles should not encourage doubt on your part. They are a segue into academic and thoughtful work that you will do. We are, as students and as people, consumers by nature.[8] Merging what you consume into an academic endeavor is a brilliant way to grow and explore. Don't be afraid. Write your own work, and explore subject areas that appeal to you, that challenge you, and that educate you. Your educational experience deserves to be original. We all start out not knowing what we're doing. The goal is to enter new territory feeling like this all the time: on the brink of discovery, nearing knowledge we didn't previously have, and allowing for others to bask in this experience with us.[9] In this way, you become a scholar, a researcher, and a thinker beyond measure. Good for you. Get going.[10]

©Alexey Stiop/Shutterstock, Inc.

SUGGESTED MATERIALS

Albert, Arthur and Greg Beeman, dirs. *The Wonder Years: Seasons 1–6.* Netflix. *Netflix.com* Web. 2015.

Goldsmith, Kenneth. "It's Not Plagiarism. In the Digital Age, It's Repurposing." *The Chronicle of Higher Education. chronicle.com* 11 Sept. 2011. Web.

   Link: http://chronicle.com/article/Uncreative-Writing/128908/

---. *Uncreative Writing: Managing Language in the Digital Age.* New York: Columbia University Press, 2011. Print.

OWL at Purdue. "MLA Formatting and Style Guide." *owl.english.purdue.edu* 2015. Web.

   Link: https://owl.english.purdue.edu/owl/resource/747/01/

Walker, Janice. "Everything Changes, or Why MLA Isn't (Always) Right." *Writing Spaces: Readings on Writing.* 2 (2011): 257–69.

   Link online: http://wac.colostate.edu/books/writingspaces2/walker--everything-changes.pdf

---

8. To prove this to you, try listing everything you have consumed so far today. Unless you're reading this early in the morning, which might be unlikely, you have consumed something. What is it?

9. For real, if you have not stopped this chapter by now to watch *The Wonder Years*, I feel bad for you. You are missing out on the beauty of Fred Savage and of being alive, truly alive. Go.

10. Well, hold up, come back. Read the rest of this book. Use the white space on the following page to draw how the first episode of *The Wonder Years* made you feel. Then, we can move to Chapter 11.

CHAPTER 11

Letting It Go: Page Lengths, Word Counts, Number of Sources, and Thesis Statements

I'm a sophomore in college. I live in a suite with six women, and my computer sits on a desk in a room I share with my best friend. I am writing a paper, absently, about a book we've just finished in one of my English classes. The paper is supposed to be five pages long. I'm on page four, and I have said every last thing I want to say in these four pages (this is rare, but it happens). My roommate is at her desk, studying.

"What else can I say about this book?" I ask her.

She's a computer science major. She stares at me.

I decide to look up more research about my topic. I pull quotes, and I cite, and I cite, and I end up looking like an idiot. All this is filler to reach five pages. I liked my conclusion, so I move it to the end, right after the last quote. Now, the conclusion doesn't fit or relate to the research. That's fine. No one will care.

Well, it turns out English professors care about what you say and write. In the margins, notes in red appear on my paper, back in my possession a week later:

How does this relate? What is the point of this quote? Why does this matter to the thesis?

I know how to revise this paper: I have to take out everything I added on page five. I do this. I add a few extended discussions of my own ideas that actually do relate to the **thesis statement** (the focus of the paper stated in the introduction). I turn the paper back for a revision grade, despite the page length not quite reaching five full pages.

And there it is, an A. Comments now read:

Good point. Nice transition. Helpful example here.

The length mattered less than the content. This lesson I learned over and over again at SUNY Geneseo. My professors, especially as I advanced in coursework, cared far less about if and when I reached a page length requirement, and far more about the quality of what I was writing. In thinking through ideas without the handcuffs of a length requirement, I was able to see that I was a writer, blooming. I did have ideas. I could articulate them. With fewer restraints, my writing blossomed.

©Anton Petrus/Shutterstock, Inc.

The concept of page lengths and word counts comes from standardization within English departments. Because English classes each cover different content and territory, a way to measure the work you accomplish in class becomes page lengths and quantity. Could each English teacher have students produce, say, 20 pages of polished (finished) prose? In seeking a standard practice, length and number or words written (word count) became the benchmark for writers. But the truth is, we also teach **writing style.** Writing style means how you use language as a writer. Are you descriptive? Lengthy or wordy? Active? Are you concise and to the point? Direct? All the ways in which you select words and put them together is what your specific writing style is. Each writer has a writing style, even if you don't believe this yet. This is how we detect plagiarism—when a writer deviates from his or her writing style, we notice. Writing style plays a major role in how long or short your papers will be.

Writing Style Quiz

Answer the questions below, and then tally up your answers.

1. In my writing, my focus is usually about:
   a. My thoughts.
   b. Action and scene.
   c. Research.

2. In most of my writing for my classes, I tend to:
   a. Write about my feelings.
   b. Describe plot or events.
   c. Write about fact-based material.

3. If given the choice to write about myself or something not focused on myself, I usually choose:
   a. Myself.
   b. Something related to me somehow.
   c. A topic unrelated to me that interests me.

4. In my writing, the majority of paragraphs are:
   a. About internal reflection and thoughts.
   b. About detailed events.
   c. About facts and research.

5. When I do research for a draft, I focus on:
   a. Stating how the research relates to me.
   b. Showing how the research enhances my ideas.
   c. Presenting as much research as possible.

6. If I have to choose one word to describe most of my current writing, it is:
   a. Emotional.
   b. Detailed.
   c. Factual.

7. An ideal paper assignment is:
   a. A personal narrative.
   b. An investigation into a topic.
   c. A report.

A: 1
B: 1
C: 5

Now, count how many As, Bs, and Cs you have.

Mostly As:

Reflective, internal writing style. Your writing tends to focus on internal feelings and thoughts, and describing how you felt at the time. Your writing style might shift tone depending on your emotional attachment to the topic: you might shift from humor to a morose or sorrowful tone depending on your thoughts about the topic you are describing. You pay attention to specific word choice and if a word accurately describes the moment.

Watch for: letting your reader know where the reflection comes from; being aware that you have to explain events to the audience.

Mostly Bs:

Detailed, descriptive writing style. Your writing tends to focus on events, specific and methodical details, and attention to transitions. Your writing style is consistent in voice. Your writing tends to focus on communicating the message through concrete and specific information. When writing, you pay attention to sequences, showing your reader a clear picture of the topic, and being thorough by adding very specific pieces of information. You like balanced prose and accuracy.

Watch for: having overly detailed writing, repeating yourself, and not evaluating the details.

Mostly Cs:

Technical, fact-based writing style. Your writing tends to focus on factual information that is able to be proven. Your writing is declarative, to the point, and concise. You tend to report information. Your writing is not biased, and you tend to give information in a very clear, general way for any reader to understand it. You are thorough and formal.

Watch for: not giving context or a basis for the research, not discussing what the research means, and not adding your own voice to the writing.

When you have a sense of your writing style, you can use this to your advantage. If you're a factual writer, you will be effective when stating a premise and proving it, most likely, with airtight, concise reasoning. If you're descriptive, you can use specific language to enhance main points and draw your reader in with detailed scenes. But get to know what type of writer you naturally are—this might influence classes you take, your major, and your career choices, because how we use language informs us of who we are and what we value.

In my own English Composition classes, I do not assign page lengths or word counts. I am fully aware that these are real requirements to be met in the writing and publishing world—many times, I have had to reach a specific length or pare back an essay submitted for publication because of a word count. Word counts mandate that there's a level playing field. I argue, though, that by the time I have accepted that I am a writer enough to submit my work for publication, then the playing field is green grass and cool breezes—what I mean by this is that I have already established that I am in a pool with others who consider themselves writers. In Composition I, while I encourage all students to consider themselves writers, many do not. Many are scared of writing, or vulnerable, and have had downfalls because they had great ideas but not enough thoughts to make it to page seven. Page seven is bunk.

I do not advocate for ignorant writing, though. I advocate for the most autonomous writing experience you, the student, can have. And having a sense of real agency with your work means you should start to get the hang of knowing when your work is and is not finished. If, say, you have written an eight-page narrative (this happens all the time), but I assigned a paper with the guideline of five to seven pages, you will cut something out. Maybe, tragically, you will cut out what is necessary for the paper to soar. I don't want you to cut it out. I want you to experience a soaring, finished paper.

The downside to not having page lengths can be that students do not learn where to cut material, or how to edit, and what needs to go. Often the precious work is left in when we know that the precious, most favored work needs to be taken out for advancement. Still, letting the guideline of the length dictate the content is unsupportive of the true writing process. The writer, you, first, needs to make choices about what needs to stay and what can go. Once you can make these decisions, then editing and revising to meet guidelines on length will be much easier, tactical, and purposeful. These choices are the ones you need to make. A brutal experience is one in which you lose vital content because you went over the length requirement and cut all the successful material out. That's a real loss.

When I stopped assigning page lengths in Composition classes, guess what happened? Students' writing improved. Immediately. Students' work was polished, confident, finished work. Students' work was coherent. Students' writing now didn't leave things out because of length requirements, and the writing didn't have filler taking up space. The work was purposeful, unified, and work that students believed in—because they made the choices about content. The more agency you have, especially at the start of the writing process, the more engaged with the work you will be.

If you have **timed writing** in class, or writing started and completed during class time, length might be on your mind here, too. When my students craft writing done in class (we call it in-class writing), at the start of a semester, some students ask, "How long does this have to be?" I say, in response, "As long as it needs to be." This gives you freedom to concentrate on the writing. And often, this in-class writing becomes pieces of a draft because the work was specific, focused, quality work. Worry less about how long and more about what the work does, says, and means.

©MorganStudio/Shutterstock, Inc.

Critical thinking (thinking about a subject beyond the obvious answers) is enhanced with agency. Some worry that, without page lengths, we are allowing you, as student writers, to toss off a paper without needing to include X number of sources or have X number of pages. Put another way, some worry that if you are no longer forced to write more to make the length requirement, you lose the critical thinking portion of the paper. You have to find ways to make it to page eight, so finding more research, or reasons, or scenes, will help. Except, without the agency of knowing why you're writing more, you lose the exercise of writing with purpose. If your purpose is to meet the bottom of page eight, your purpose is lost. If your purpose is to cover all your reasons for your premise, with research and logic, then it's entirely your choice when the paper comes to an end. Knowing when your work is done is one of the most powerful pieces of the writing process that a writer can and will have. Stripping you of this choice removes the critical thinking from the writing itself. And a word of warning: don't sell yourself short by simply ending a paper when you feel like it. Avoid only writing what you think you can to get by; this wastes your time. Writing less than a finished paper doesn't help you learn to write. Just because there's no length requirement doesn't mean to leave out whatever you can to get the paper done. Your professor will look for, and ask for, the rest. You owe yourself the practice of writing a full paper.

In Chapter 10, we covered research. The counting standard for the number of sources used in a paper mimics the page length or word count benchmarks when it comes to assessing our courses. Many Composition classes ask or even require a set number of outside sources in a paper. This practice, however, misses the agency that could become part of your research and writing processes: shoving sources into a document doesn't inherently make the document better. Sometimes, too many sources take away from the writing you are capable of doing, or overwhelms the text. Sometimes, students have some excellent sources, and cannot find more, so they end up shoving filler research into the text—sound familiar? Knowing where appropriate research fits within your own writing is the point, not counting the sources in the text. Unified writing happens when you have the agency to decide where outside research fits, and to make this research meaningful to your work. Counting for counting's sake is not an effective benchmark for you. If you run short on sources, and believe you have enough, speak to your professor. See what happens.

Another common item on the checklist of a Composition I paper is the **thesis statement**, or the written focus of what your paper or project will be about. The thesis statement, often in paragraph one, is meant to be stated on the first page of your text so the reader knows the focus of the work. The thesis sets the stage for the document's content and tells us the purpose of the document. Many professors use different terms for the thesis statement; they all mean the same thing. If you see, on an assignment sheet, these words, they mean thesis statement:

- central focus
- goal of the paper
- premise of the paper
- main idea
- main focus
- primary focus
- aim

A major rule to break is to omit this piece of a thesis statement: "In this paper, I will . . ." Don't hand your reader this. Trust your writing, and the ability of the reader, to locate the goal of the paper naturally.

If you're unsure what your thesis is and already have some writing done, write down the main point of each paragraph you already have. Collect these main ideas, and write the introduction. By finding what the ideas have in common, you can create a thesis statement that covers all the work you've written thus far. Writing an introduction last is a time-saver, and a way to focus your work. When you have an idea for the thesis, write it down. Try to give your papers titles. If you have a title that is not something like, "Unit II Paper," but instead is something like, "Isolation in Memoir-Writing," you have a very clear focus and that's your thesis.

Thesis Statement Exercise: How to Locate A Thesis Statement

If you start with an idea for the paper, fill in the circle in the middle first. If you have many ideas about the assignment, write these in the white spaces first.

An idea you want to work out   Key information to include

What connects
all the pieces =
your thesis

An example of your ideas   Alternative perspectives

Details you want to include

Fill in as many of these pieces as you can. Once you have the circle filled in, you have a working thesis statement.

A thesis statement does not have to list three main points. In fact, don't count the points you will cover in a paper. Just have good, effective, meaningful points. The **five-paragraph essay**, or the prescriptive formula of an introductory paragraph with your thesis, three body paragraphs, and a concluding paragraph, is outdated and limiting. Three is not a magical number if you have two awesome main points, or four. Work out your ideas for meaning, not for numbers. Think hard about what you want when writing a paper, because your goals shape your outcome.

Writing Expectations: Being Autonomous

What are your own expectations for yourself as a writer? From this chapter, I hope you have identified your writing style, or started to. Now, ask yourself these questions to see what motivates you to write.

- What do you hope to gain by writing in this course?

- What will be common types of writing for you after this course?

- What scares you about writing?

- What do you avoid when writing?

- What types of writing appeal to you? (Remember, writing includes film and television scripts, such as comedy, drama, and fantasy; investigative journalism; memoir work; cookbooks; etc.).

- Do you wish you could write like someone else? Who?

Once you have some answers to these questions, allow your writing to move in these directions. Try writing like a writer you admire. Try writing in the genre that you will write at work, or down the road when you're through with this class, for practice. Face what you have been avoiding. You'll have purpose this way.

All writers have insecurities. Mine is being too wordy, and being too detailed. Being overly detailed is akin to telling a too-long story and someone rolling their eyes, or not paying attention any longer. I do this to my husband, Dan, all the time. Once I decided to work on being more succinct, the length of some of my essays changed, shortened, and the work got decidedly better. Dan got happier.

©Csaba Peterdi/Shutterstock, Inc.

You're in charge of your writing. If you do have restrictions on word counts, pages written, sources used, make sure you believe in the work. Talk to your professor about form versus content: is it more important that the document reach a standard on length and number counts, or more important that the work is solid, effective, advancing? It is possible to achieve both outcomes, likely if you discuss your options with your professor. Draft as much as you can. Put the draft away for as long as you can. Return to it, see it again, add or subtract. Once you are in the process of adding and cutting, you're in writer territory: you have arrived. Every writer makes changes. Knowing what yours are and why they are is the difference between gunning for a grade and becoming a writer and thinker. The choice is yours—and it always should be.

SUGGESTED MATERIALS

Brown, Amanda Christy and Katherine Schulten. "Writing Rules! Advice from the Times on Writing Well." *The Learning Network: The New York Times* learning.blogs.nytimes.com 20 Sept. 2012. Web.

Link: http://learning.blogs.nytimes.com/2012/09/20/writing-rules-advice-from-the-new-york-times-on-writing-well/comment-page-2/?_r=0

Robinson, Ken. "How Schools Kill Creativity: TED Talk." *ted.com* Feb. 2006. Web.

Link: http://www.ted.com/talks/ken_robinson_says_schools_kill_creativity

Solomon, Andrew. "The Middle of Things: Advice for Young Writers." *The New Yorker newyorker.com* 11 Mar. 2015. Web.

Link: http://www.newyorker.com/books/page-turner/the-middle-of-things-advice-for-young-writers?intcid=mod-most-popular

Toor, Rachel. "Bad Writing and Bad Thinking." *The Chronicle of Higher Education chronicle.com* 15 Apr. 2010. Web.

Link: http://chronicle.com/article/Bad-WritingBad-Thinking/65031/

CHAPTER 12

Taking Risks: Our Spheres, Identity, and "Scary" Course Material

I'm on my way to class. I'm nervous, which is unusual unless it's the first day, which it isn't. It's the middle of the semester. I am rehearsing a bit of what I will say today in class. It's my Spheres day; I am feeling vulnerable.

The particular class that I am walking into is loud. They sit in factions, and the factions don't really talk to each other. This bothers me. I have decided to present my Spheres to them today—something I have not yet done—and see if we can get to a place of being human. At some point in every class, I present my Spheres.

When I get to class, I put three columns on the board. "These," I say, "are pieces of a narrative of a senior in college." Then I write all of this on the board:

EDUCATION:	PROFESSIONAL:	PERSONAL:
• 3.8 GPA • Major: Communication • Minors: Dance, Creative Writing • Has scholarships • Admitted into graduate school	• Writes for national magazine • Admitted to graduate program • Starts first campus magazine • Internship leads to NYS Emmy	

At this point, I ask the students what they think of this person. "Accomplished," someone says. "Awesome," says another. Someone makes a joke about being better than he is. I turn back to the board and fill in the third column, personal information:

EDUCATION:	PROFESSIONAL:	PERSONAL:
• 3.8 GPA • Major: Communication • Minors: Dance, Creative Writing • Has scholarships • Admitted into graduate school	• Writes for national magazine • Starts first campus magazine • Internship leads to NYS Emmy	• Starts dating a guy • Enters into an abusive relationship • At the end, he attempts to hit her with own car • He comes after her with hammer • He is arrested • He steals all her money

The students usually gasp, or at least pay more attention at this point.

"This," I say, pointing to the board, "is my narrative."

Then the questions start. My students ask how I met this guy and what happened.

In a nutshell, I tell them this:

I met this guy when I was a senior in college. He was charming: a bit older, had grown up in and out of America. He was handsome and pursued me, relentlessly. I should have seen this as a red flag, but I didn't. Instead, I found him charming, persistent.

This guy slowly started showing signs of violence. Once, when we were at a bar, I started dancing with my ex-boyfriend, and this guy got furious; I got scared. I went into the bathroom and he followed me, punching the paper towel dispenser; it hung askew off the wall. I was terrified. We agreed to leave the bar. At home, he continued to get angry and punched a hole in my bedroom door. The police were called, and he fled on foot.

I didn't break up with him, though. I moved out of the house I lived in with five other women, and they stopped speaking to me when I continued to date him. The abuse got worse. Eventually, it ended with the guy coming after me.

At this point, students start verbally processing some of this. They acknowledge that my story disrupts their understanding of me, of who they thought I was—nice, congenial blonde girl from the East Coast, someone who laughs a lot. I am these things, and, I say, I am also a survivor of domestic violence. "But you're so nice," one says. "How did this happen?" asks everyone. They want to know how it ended, so we pick up here.

After two years, when I was in my first year of graduate school, I knew I had to leave this guy. We were living in an isolated lake house. I told him I was moving out. We had people over, and he got angry (this was a pattern), and he threw a chair through the windows on the second floor of the rental house. Glass went everywhere. I left with a guy I was casually dating (This muddles the story, but I have to be honest; I constantly tell my students to be honest).

The guy came after us in my car, and, when he spotted us on the back rural roads, he gunned the engine in an attempt to hit me on the passenger side where I sat. Missing, he hit another car (I think), and a guardrail (I know). The car was heavily damaged, but this didn't stop him from driving it into the lake and reporting it stolen.

I continued on to a house where the guy-I-had-been-casually-dating lived. My ex eventually found us by driving to the house in our second car. He got into the house wielding a hammer. He came after me, someone called the police. He was handcuffed. I was put into police protection in the back of one of the police cars in the driveway, shaking. As my ex walked by, he spit at my window.

I tell my students all of this. It's risky, yes, and it's valid too. I ask my students to share their lives with me through their narrative work and through their class discussions. I want to meet my students in the middle place, that vulnerable, honest space, because they deserve to understand who I am, too.

This Spheres exercise opens up all sorts of conversations, depending on the class. Sometimes, we focus on how students have witnessed other abusive relationships and how, or if, to intervene or say something. Sometimes, this leads to a conversation about seeing red flags; students sometimes identify they are in unhealthy relationships. Almost every time I present my narrative, we talk about identity construction, and how a disruptive event or act can interrupt and re-channel how we form our own identities, and how certain events or life experiences can disrupt others' expectations of who we are. This moment helps us in all Composition I units because it addresses social and psychological territory, narrative risks, providing information, and potentially addressing how to research aspects of our experiences.

Importantly, this presentation lets students get to know me more deeply, and this risk is worth taking—they trust me, and I trust them with my narrative. It's a mutually beneficial experience, I hope.

©Chris Howey/Shutterstock, Inc.

Your Spheres: How Do You Define and Understand Your Identity?

Think about who you are right now. Select from the list below, or come up with your own Spheres categories that most specifically get to the heart of what has contributed to your identity.

Considerations:

- Education
- Professional Life
- Personal Life
- Where You Grew Up
- Family
- Relationships
- Friendships
- Trauma
- Where You Live Now

> Pick three or name three of your own making. Put them into three lists, and itemize what you need to in order to list the most important pieces.
>
> When you're done, share these lists with a partner during class. When it's your partner's turn, listen fully.
>
> This should open you up to hear and learn more about each other in class; this risk offers a huge reward: understanding the people in this class more deeply, and being vulnerable.

Think hard about your spheres. How do they inform your reactions to people in class when they speak? How do the spheres inform you of why you respond to reading material a certain way? By considering what has contributed to who you are, you're doing the work of analysis. You are also taking a risk to look inward, reflect, and share yourself with the class.

Once we've done the work of listening to, and processing, my story, I re-draw it into actual spheres, which is where the name originates. I want students to see how our spheres overlap and inform pieces of who we are. I draw three intertwined circles and decide what has influenced each circle:

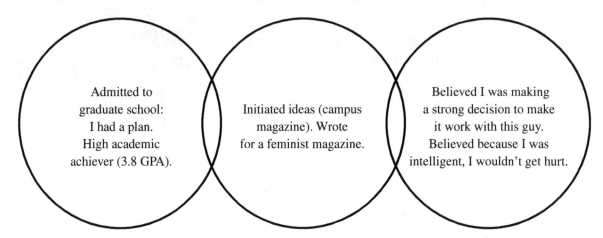

These spheres overlap in many ways. Of most importance to me are the paradoxes of who I was (and am). Seeing these discrepancies informs students that we disrupt our expected identities all the time. Being mindful of this, being aware of how our qualities push and pull our behaviors, helps us recognize our own humanity, and where we can improve. My life spheres inform how I teach, and I want this to be transparent. Your life spheres overlap and inform your identity and how you behave as a student.

What also contributes to your identity construction are your **values**, **ethics**, and **morals**. In class, we put these terms on the board. Let's try.

Values: how do you define values? Add your definition here: _____

_____.

List three values that you have:

1.

2.

3.

Now, move to **ethics**. Add your definition of ethics here:

_____.

Lastly, **morals**. How do you distinguish morals from values and ethics? Define what you think morals are here:

_____ .

As a class, it's valuable to have this conversation and get clear, or try to, about what these elements of an individual are, and as a society, what we consider these terms to mean.

Usually, my classes arrive at definitions that look somewhat like this:

Values: Things and people that you cherish. Examples: time, my mom, my dog, money.

Ethics: An agreed-upon set of social behaviors that are acceptable. Examples: helping someone when they fall, not cheating on a test, giving an iPhone that you found on the bus to Lost and Found.

Morals: Your private, personal set of beliefs. Examples: your stance on abortion, your stance on a political party, your set of religious beliefs.

These are floating definitions. You and your class can come up with original answers. This helps understand where everyone in class fits within these constructs and it takes a risk to talk through these very personal pieces of identity. It's risky to share in discussion—for me, too, sometimes. But it's worth it because you engage with a level of respect and trust that helps advance our thinking about one another, and our care for one another. This also fosters critical thinking throughout.

Your values, ethics, and morals come into play when you write a paper. Ideally, your morals require you to write your own paper, instead of plagiarizing. Your values will dictate paper topics, and sometimes, even who you find credible when researching. Your values also come into play when writing about what you believe in or think is real or true.

Taking a risk writing a paper with a topic that presents a stance that's different from your instructor's is a great example of a possibly rewarding educational experience. I once had a student worry because he wanted to write an anti-feminist paper, and he acknowledged that he knew I was a feminist. I told him that didn't matter and to write the paper. The exercise was a valuable one because the student had a very clear sense of audience awareness and this helped shape his arguments. He worked hard to be logical and persuasive, and he succeeded. This is a risky practice for students who are fearful of being down-graded for opposing values or positions. We've covered this before in this book, but the risk of it is worth discussing again: if you are fearful, talk to your professor first. Ask about the topic and your stance. Having this conversation enriches your education. And if you are ready to then go forth, good for you—having a deliberate, challenging topic and audience will help your writing grow.

I once had a student who wrote a very dynamic paper—until I reached a part where women were objectified. I paused. I had two responses: the professor response as the grader, and the human response as a woman. This portion of the paper did contribute to the narrative—it could not detract from the grade. So, in the end comments, there were two types: a grade explanation and a human reaction. In the grade explanation, I explained why the paper was an A. In the human reaction, I noted that there was a portion of the work that seemed to objectify women. This led to a discussion with the student—he wasn't aware he'd presented the scene the way I saw it. We talked about his views, and he wanted to make sure I knew that he respected women. I believed him. And he trusted me to grade his work, not his morals and values.

The issue of taking risks with written material spills into a conversation about assigned readings. First of all, read them, even when, especially when, they challenge you. When I assign, "Where I Slept," by Stephen Elliott, students are a bit shocked that Elliott was using drugs and homeless at age 14. When I assign "The Love of My Life," by Cheryl Strayed (see Chapter 4's reading list for this essay), students are sometimes appalled. Some even drop my class. It's the first essay I assign in the narrative unit. In it, Strayed uses drugs, has a controversial medical procedure done, grieves, and has a ton of sex. The point of the essay is not to shock you—but if that happens, we have to talk about it.

Reading work that challenges you is a productive experience because it starts to pinpoint areas of identity that might not emerge if you were not challenged, and it asks you to investigate your responses instead of ignoring them. I suggest to my students, and to you, to mark the places where you feel most challenged, repelled, bored, or angry (reactive) to the text you're reading. This will help you understand what material, and its presentation, draws the reaction. Then, we will talk about why this is happening.

Don't be afraid of difficult topics in writing. In my Honors Composition I course, we just finished reading the memoir *Lucky*, by Alice Sebold. Before starting the book, we had a discussion about everyone's comfort level reading about rape—because the first 16 pages of the memoir are a direct, brutal account of Sebold being raped by a stranger on the last day of her freshman year at Syracuse. When students returned to class to talk about these pages, they were ready. In both classes, students had a wide variety of reactions and we had to work through them all. Because we had already done some identity construction work, the space was safe to disclose what students really felt and thought. There were disagreements about Alice's actions. We argued logically, moving into territory that is usually ignored when we talk about rape victims. One student even stated, "I'm glad we're talking about this. Nobody ever does."

This memoir led to discussions about gender and students' feelings of safety in relationship to their own genders. We discussed issues related to victim-blaming and crimes against women in America; students began doing research about college rape cases and reportage. We began to investigate media responses and media coverage of rape cases, and we looked hard at resources for victims of trauma. All of this came out of a memoir that most were fearful to begin reading.

I live in Kansas, a state that has initiated a bill (not yet a practicable law) that restricts K–12 reading material in classes that is either pornographic or determined to be too dangerous, harmful, or risky for students to read. One legislator remarked that work by Toni Morrison would be prohibited (if you are not familiar with Toni Morrison, drop this book and go find one of hers. I'm serious).

Even if you don't like reading, this is a dangerous initiative. I have students who resist difficult topics because the work makes them uncomfortable. I don't assign challenging work to make you feel scared or anxious. However, the point of college is not to skate by, reading your favorite easy book over and over again. A point of this class, for you, is to identify what challenges you, and to understand why. These answers aren't easy, but they're valuable. If I had resisted reading Jeanette Winterson's novels in an English class, I would not have identified that I was challenged by extreme femininity and extreme sexual openness. Because I waded through the material, I opened to it, and learned about alternatives to the relationships I understood in my own life. I saw a bigger part of humanity.

What Challenges You?

Put a checkmark next to each topic that challenges you or might make you uncomfortable. At the end, write two topics not on the list to add.

_____ Sexual relationships   _____ Assault / violence

_____ Drug use / abuse   _____ Sexual assault / sexual violence

_____ Family struggles   _____ Political discourse

_____ Issues of gender   _____ Issues of LGBTQIA communities

_____ Issues of race   _____ Issues of class

_____ Domestic abuse / domestic violence   _____ Relationship dysfunction

_____   _____

If you are willing, select one topic that challenges you—one item that has a checkmark next to it without a doubt, and either write a paper about why this topic is challenging to you, or find an article or a book on this topic and evaluate the material, explaining why the book did or did not help you reorganize your difficulty with this topic.

The point of any challenge is not simply to overcome it, but to learn from it. I didn't simply survive my experiences with my abuser. I understood, with a lot of recovery and resources, what a healthy relationship should look like and why I (and you) should expect that. In meeting my husband, I was able to put these pieces into place to move forward, recognizing and fostering a healthy, safe relationship.

In my challenging class, after I presented the Spheres exercise, students hugged me. Some revealed to me their own struggles. One student, a faction-leader, revealed some of his own familial difficulties that helped explain his behavior; he began exploring why he wanted to be in control, and discovered, by the end of the semester, that some of his overlap with control and academic success was a lack of control with certain unhealthy family relationships. His discovery, entirely his own, was jump-started by his willingness to explore who he was, in some Spheres, and how the Spheres held influence. Educated risk-taking will benefit you in the classroom, in your writing, and in your life. At work, if you say yes to something that, at first, challenges you or makes you afraid, you're engaging with a new piece of the world. If you've done some reflective writing about who you are, you will be able to navigate this challenge with skill. I was so proud of my class after the Spheres presentation. The dynamic shifted, and the factions disappeared. Whatever was holding them back dissolved into exploration and kindness. All it took was a bit of a leap, some honesty, and a mutual exchange of trust. Now, your turn.

©Romolo Tavani/Shutterstock, Inc.

SUGGESTED MATERIALS

Baker, Katie J.M. "College Defends Removing Student Over 'Disruptive' Rape Remarks." *BuzzFeed* buzzfeed.com. 19 Mar. 2015.

Link: http://www.buzzfeed.com/katiejmbaker/college-professor-bans-student-from-class-for-his-views-on-r#.yeW522vgVE

Conti, Allie. "New Kansas Law Would Make It A Crime to Teach Sex Ed, Classical Art, and Shakespeare." *Vice* vice.vom 3 Mar. 2015. Web.

*Link:*http://www.vice.com/read/kansas-is-voting-on-a-bill-that-will-ban-any-book-that-talks-about-sex-from-public-schools

Elliott, Stephen. "Where I Slept." *Therumpus.net* 1 Apr. 2009. Web.

Link: http://therumpus.net/2009/04/where-i-slept/

McDonough, Katie. "Trigger Warnings on Campus: What the Critics Are Missing." *Salon.com* 4 Mar. 2014. Web.

Link: http://www.salon.com/2014/03/04/trigger_warnings_on_campus_what_the_critics_are_missing/

Schulevitz, Julia. "In College and Hiding from Scary Ideas." *The New York Times Sunday Review* nytimes.com. 21 Mar. 2015.

Link: http://www.nytimes.com/2015/03/22/opinion/sunday/judith-shulevitz-hiding-from-scary-ideas.html?smprod=nytcore-ipad

CHAPTER 13

On Coming Across: Establishing Tone and Voice

My first memory of hearing the word "tone" used was as a reprimand against me. I distinctly remember my mother saying, "Don't take that tone with me." It meant I was being sassy, or mouthy, or any of the other admonishments our parents have against us as we start to defy our attachments to them and become our own (sassy) people. So, I learned that having a tone was negative.

Even today, when my husband Dan and I fight (yes, this happens), we will occasionally say to one another something along the lines of, "Can you please lower your voice?" or, "Can you check your tone, please?" to recover a sense of kindness to the dialogue. If I think about it, I was taught in social situations what tone and voice mean—and why they can hurt others and ourselves when they either get out of our control or are used intentionally as weapons.

It should be said that language can be both a powerful tool and a weapon. Musician Ani DiFranco has a lot of songs about language as power, and many rhetoricians, thinkers, and writers endorse this concept. In her song, "I'm No Heroine," as an example, DiFranco sings about why she writes music: she hopes other women hear her songs and that they help women to survive. This is language seen as a tool for fostering hope and positive change. Many hip-hop artists use language in these capacities—for hope and change (see Tupac's "Changes" on this), and to instigate action against oppression (see Dr. Dre on this, especially during the LA riots). And in 2015, we have, conversely, a very damaging example of language as a weapon when a video was leaked of the University of Oklahoma SAE chapter's members chanting a racist song on a bus—it was filmed, and leaked, and led to the expulsion of two of the instigators, along with sparking a national debate about language usage. In the video, the tone of the chant, which matters, is jovial, celebratory, which contributed to how offensive it is. The **tone** is the inflection of the voices—the voices are being carried into a space of cheer. The language is not cheery—it's racist and dangerous. Combined, this became a powder keg. Tone matters—it's how your language is carried.

In my classes, we debate and go through the usual discussions about how we distinguish between tone and voice. Both are given attention when we evaluate writing—and when we evaluate how we speak to others, and how we are spoken to. **Tone** is generally easier for us to name—it's the conveyance of how you feel about your subject, your attitude toward the subject. So, when I am arguing with Dan, my tone is angry because I feel angry (like these tigers):

©Kagai19927/Shutterstock, Inc.

If you were trying to get permission from a parent to go out on a Friday night, your tone might be pleading because you really want to go out that night (maybe like this plea):

The **voice** is the carrier—literally—of the tone, and it's also the figurative way you approach language. You take a tone—angry—and your **voice**—your usual speech pattern and way of communication— is disrupted because usually you use words that send a message of kindness. In my mind, voice is the carrier of tone and the language pattern you commonly use. If you speak up and start yelling obscenities in class, and usually you're shy and quiet, we will notice both your tone shifting and how your voice is usually not filled with obscene language. In this way, we start to see that you definitely have a communication style.

Tone & Voice: A Beginning Exercise

In this short exercise, select a word that most accurately fits how you would describe each subject.

1. A dog is:
   A. Playful
   B. Dumb
   C. Too much work

2. A cat is:
   A. Cute
   B. Annoying
   C. Wily

3. A rainbow is:
   A. Beautiful
   B. Lucky
   C. A cliché

4. Roses are:
   A. Fragrant
   B. Pretty
   C. Thorny

5. A pebble is:
   A. Smooth
   B. Colorful
   C. Round

Now, with all your answers, put each subject and your accompanying descriptor into a paragraph.

For example, if these are my answers, I write: *A dog is playful. A cat is annoying. A rainbow is lucky. Roses are pretty. A pebble is smooth.* Assess your sentences. What tone comes across? Is this small paragraph using words you usually use? If so, what does this mean about your writing?

If not, what words, if given an opportunity to use your own, would you replace these with? Once you see how you use language, you can start to identify the tone you are conveying—intentionally or otherwise.

The intention of language usage is a big deal. Have you ever texted someone you know, and the tone or message came across differently than what you meant? This is a very common example of why language and tone matter—a great deal. I have a family member who sometimes likes to write emphasis with all capital letters. To me, this means she's yelling. If we see this in an email, we're likely to react in a way that's counter to the intended message. Watch. Here's an example:

Dear Sam,

Hi! How are you? I am great. We've had a lovely time planting flowers this spring. I CAN FINALLY PLANT AGAIN. IT HAS BEEN TOO LONG. I also made chili and it got colder last night—I hope the flowers don't die.

Love,

Amy

When I read this, I think, *Who has been keeping Amy from planning flowers?* And I think it in a negative way, as in, *Who has isolated Amy from gardening*? This is not intentional. Amy is just really excited to plant things. SHE IS SO EXCITED.

Miscommunication happens in texting and emailing a lot. People we write to in these capacities often grow to expect a certain voice from us. If, say, you're really sarcastic, and suddenly become maudlin and sincere, some audience members might not even believe you're being honest. This means sarcasm and humor are ingrained into your voice and your writing style. I, for example, swear a lot in emails and texts to my friends. If I write them a text one day that disrupts this voice, they doubt I am being truthful. For example, I take the commuter bus a lot from where I live to my campus to get to work. One summer day, the bus broke down and I had to figure out how to get a ride to my car at Park & Ride, about 15 minutes away from where I was stranded in 100 degree heat. My usual text would be something like, *F**ing stuck at 23rd and Haskell: stupid bus. Can anyone give me a ride?* This is my voice with my friends. If I texted them and said, *I have found myself in somewhat of a situation. The bus has dropped me off at 23rd Street and the only recourse I have is to get to my car another way. Is anyone available?*, they would think I was on LSD or having a breakdown. My writing voice, and yours, predicates expectations about what we say and write, and how we do so. Word choice, often called **diction**, helps develop your individual voice.

Your friends and family likely have expectations about your usual voice—and this changes based on context. My students expect me to have a more professional voice—I am still me, but I don't come into class swearing. Your professors likely have expectations for how you speak in class as an individual, and in other contexts, like work, friends, and family situations, expectations about your voice and tone are derived from patterns of word choice and inflection. I know a woman who usually speaks very softly and always says, "You know what I mean?" If she suddenly started shouting and declaring her opinions, this would surprise me. We develop expectations based on these speech and writing patterns.

Language Usage & Primary Source Assignment

If you're willing to investigate your patterns of word choices and tone, there are a few compelling options to experiment with and write about. These involve using people who know you as primary sources of research.

Option 1: Experimental Diction. Email a few friends or text a few people in your life whom you write to often. Use completely different words than usual. Pay attention to how the recipients respond. Follow up and ask them if this threw them off in any way, and how and why that might have changed how they interpreted your message. Reflect upon what this experiment means about your voice, tone, and diction.

Option 2: Interviews. Interview friends and people whom you write to or speak with on a regular basis. Ask them what words you commonly repeat, to describe the voice and tone you commonly use when you interact with them, and how they might describe your communication style. Reflect upon the responses and see if you agree or disagree with them.

Option 3: Film & Audio Recording. Film yourself talking causally or record yourself talking. Play it back. What inflections do you notice? What words are used most frequently or repeated? What tone is coming across here? Reflect upon what you hear.

These experiments offer new ways to see what your language and speech patterns are to actual audience members. Then, decide what you want to keep and what you want to change about these patterns. Reflect upon your common word choices and speech patterns, and write about them—and how these choices impact your writing.

A significant piece of written communication that should be addressed is in your professor's **end comments** on your work. Written or typed, these are the comments at the end of your work that the professor uses to communicate areas of strength and weakness, and areas that contributed to the grade, if one is given. The tone of these end comments matters a great deal. Have you ever had a teacher or professor write very little on your work? I had a professor in college who would only write **marginal comments,** or notes to me in the margins of the paper. They said things like, "Good point," or "Why is this example here?" I didn't feel fortified by these comments; I usually felt that I was guessing about why something was praised or what a comment referred to in the text I wrote. This tone came across as busy, uninvolved, and disengaged from my work. The professor was fantastic, and I never asked for clarification because I was scared to. Don't do this. As we've already addressed, advocate for yourself and follow up if marginal or end comments either don't exist or don't make sense. Always ask. This will help the professor understand how her own comments are being received.

When I was in graduate school and a graduate teaching assistant (GTA), we were required during our first semester to show our advisor a sample of graded papers so he could see our end comments. In class, our advisor addressed how many students' comments had a disrespectful, caustic, or frustrated tone. The GTAs were unaware of their tone—they were teachers, hoping to help. But they were likely scaring and intimidating students, which is bad. Intervening shaped and changed this—be the intervener. Your work and the feedback you receive matters.

Commenting on others' work is a skill that we need to develop. When asked to read other students' work in class during peer review situations, students almost always either are afraid to offer anything negative ("Looks great!" comments are frequent and unhelpful), or students think the point is to locate all the flaws and list them ("This thesis statement is boring; your logic is flawed, this example doesn't make sense;" these kinds of comments happen, and they can be hurtful). In classes, I remind students to treat others' work as they want their work to be handled—with kindness and thoughtfulness. Offer a strength first. Each writer has one—find it. Then, find the most pervasive, more important pieces that need work. Offer suggestions. In this positive constructive criticism, we model how to make our work better while celebrating that it already has something working. This skill will help in positive work environments also—tremendously.

Many students struggle with the barrier from speech to the written work. I hear students say all the time, "I can say what I mean, but when I go to write it down, it's different or I can't get it right." I also hear students say, "This isn't what I mean, but it's close." What happens between our speech and our writing worlds? They're two different ways of using language. In speech, your tone carries weight for you—if you're trying to make a funny point, in speech, you can pace the joke with pauses. In writing, you need to make pacing part of the words chosen, or the punctuation achieves this pacing—that's difficult work. Think about results and what words will get you to these results. If you can speak your idea aloud, you can write it. Tutors are often taught to write what students say and repeat it to the student—this is what can be transcribed and turned into writing that expresses exactly what you said and meant.

Comedians are adept at showing why tone and voice matter to the message. The show *Key & Peele*, on Comedy Central, uses pacing, voice changes, and tone as part of their sketches. In one particular sketch that I show my students, called "Meegan Come Back," they replicate a typical scene of a heterosexual couple fighting late at night after going out together. The skit rests on stereotypical gender roles—the woman refuses to go home with her boyfriend out of anger, and keeps repeating, "No," while the boyfriend dutifully tries to give her her jacket. It sounds boring, but it's wildly funny because of each actor's tone and voice. The humor is in the language, surely, and also in the tone and voice to carry the frustration and anger during the fight.

A different route into using tone and voice is through visual media. More and more, visual media is allowed into Composition work—like a digital narrative as an assignment, or personal drawings to express the emotional value of the message or position in a paper. Photographs, for example, carry a tone and voice. Take this image of a sunset.

What do you see? What emotions come forward when looking at this?

Now see this image of a sunset.

©KonstantinChristian/Shutterstock, Inc.

What do you see now? Are these the same emotions as the first photo? Probably not. Just like composing details in your written work, the details in the images cohere to form a message in the photos. All of this is intentional, and thus part of composition. As Dan says, tone is the set design of a movie, and the voice is in the acting.

Allie Brosh is a blogger who became famous for creating her blog that's now a book of the same name: *Hyperbole and a Half.* In her book, she writes serious essays about being severely depressed, and she also writes hilarious essays about her life (dogs and candy take up a lot of the narratives). She uses Apple software to draw herself, sometimes as a kid, and to draw the narrative moments that are emotional. The drawings carry the humor or the sorrow expressed. You can see, for instance, the hilarity in Allie as a kid in her wide-open eyes in some of the essays, or the amusing stupidity of her dog when it's drawn with its mouth hanging open. Her writing is detailed, too, and works to tell the stories and to develop her voice. Her artwork shows the emotions and sets the tone.

Experimenting with Form: Composition Assignments

To work with tone and voice, select an option to synthesize format and content into a new, original work.

1. **Artwork.** Write a paper about a subject of your choice, using your own artwork (hand-drawn or with software) to enhance the tone and voice.

2. **Photography.** Select or take a series of photographs that develop a specific tone and voice—and a selective message for the viewer. Write captions when applicable.

3. **Podcast.** Make a podcast, where you record your voice and other sounds, to tell a story. Whatever option you select, pay attention to the tone coming across. Show the draft of the product to other people and gauge their reactions—are the reactions what you hoped for? If not, find ways to achieve this goal. If the answer is yes, congratulations.

When you start to pay attention to your tone and voice, you will be more aware of it in many situations—and many important ones, like a job interview, a meeting, a difficult conversation. This awareness will also give you the freedom and responsibilities that come with it—to be respectful, and to develop specific emotional reactions to your work from people. The more you are aware of tone and voice, the better your writing gets because the writing is from you as a human, not you as a robot trying to get an A. You can get an A and develop your voice as a writer. Think about it: no two presidents of the United States have the same emotional value when they give speeches. Each has his own repeated words, and each has his own tone to deliver his messages. This is true for you, too. It's why your tone and voice are like snowflakes and fingerprints: no two patterns are alike. Cherish yours, embrace yours, and work on them as you keep writing. In this way, your communication will advance, not just in this class, but in your life.

©Ariena/Shutterstock, Inc.

SUGGESTED MATERIALS

Brosh, Allie. *Hyperbole and a Half.* Blog. 2009. Web.

   Link: http://www.hyperboleandahalf.blogspot.com/

Key & Peele. "Meegan Come Back." *Key & Peele.* Comedy Central. 7 Nov. 2012. *YouTube*

   Link: https://www.youtube.com/watch?v=eirBtt7wIDU

Lee, Kate Kiefer. "Tone and Voice: What's the Difference?" *Forbes forbes.com* 12 Sept. 2012. Web.

   Link: http://www.forbes.com/sites/katelee/2012/09/12/voice-and-tone-whats-the-difference/

Norman, Avital N. "Mom and Pop Culture: An Interview with Ani DiFranco." *Bitch Media bitchmagazine.org* 22. Dec. 2011. Web.

   Link: http://bitchmagazine.org/post/mom-pop-culture-an-interview-with-ani-difranco

Svrluga, Susan. "OU: Frat Members Learned Racist Chant at National SAE Leadership Event." *Washington Post washingtonpost.com* 27 Mar. 2015. Web.

   Link: http://www.washingtonpost.com/news/grade-point/wp/2015/03/27/ou-investigation-sae-members-learned-racist-chant-at-national-leadership-event/

CHAPTER 14

Student Crisis, Mental Health, Suicide, and Disclosure

It's the start of a fall semester, and I am teaching a Composition I class. In the corner are two guys who will not stop talking. As we go around the room, I understand why they're so chatty: they're best friends. One even discloses on his First Day Sheet that he's leaning on the other to hold him accountable for coming to class.

As the semester moves along, the two become a classroom hit. One says something funny; the other backs it up with something funnier. I learn that other students in the class went to high school with these two. They're well-liked. One, in particular, J., is a bit moody, whereas his counterpart, B., is light. J. emerges as a deep thinker, a very serious student who loves writing and thinking about difficult, complex ideas. B. gives his ideas bounce and humor. Together, on some days, they almost run some of the lesson plans and include everyone in the discussions. It's a class made for each other.

Until life interrupts. J. stops coming to class. Then he returns, almost incommunicative. I report his behavior to a First Alert system the counseling center has on our campus to check in with him. He comes in late one day for an in-class writing day. He writes frantically the entire time. When the time's up, he rushes out of the room without handing anything in. I go into the hallway after him, but I don't find him.

That was the last time I ever saw J.

In class on Friday, I notice J. is missing, as is B. Usually, I see one of them, so this is a bit alarming. In my second class, a high school friend of J.'s and B.'s comes up to me and says, "They found J.'s body in the park." I pull him into the hallway. "What?"

The student tells me what he knows, which is not a lot. I somehow manage to convince myself that this isn't real. I call my husband Dan after, in the October sunshine outside on the quad. I start to cry. I believe it's real.

It's real.

J. committed suicide. I learn more after—at the funeral, and when B. comes into the classroom and weep-talks through how he's going to manage. But before all this, when I learn that the death is true, I have to tell my class.

Telling my class that J. is dead is, and will remain, one of the hardest parts of my life. Not career. Life.

Everyone in class admired and liked J., including me. B. was absent the next class. I sat on the desk as usual. People settled in and stopped talking. I pointed to the empty chair and cried my way through the news. I said things like, "I've never done this before," and "You all are important." I was so very scared that another suicide would happen—when a friend or someone close commits suicide, it can encourage the act in others. I was scared for my students' welfare.

In Matt Richtel's article "Push, Don't Crush, the Students," he notes that "Suicide clusters are relatively rare, accounting for about 5 percent of teenage suicide," and also cautions: "Experts say such clusters typically occur when suicide takes hold as a viable coping mechanism—as a deadly, irrational fashion." Seeing a student commit suicide can be a caution or an invitation. Our goal is to disinvite the prospect for students, and for each other in our classes.

I dismissed my students after this messy dialogue. One stood at the door, propping it open, his friends waiting outside.

"What you do," he said quietly, "it matters."

When someone you know dies, your world is rearranged, sometimes permanently. When you, as students, see behavior that could be classified as troubling, a question arises: what do you do?

The answer depends on many pieces: your level of comfort, your resources, and who you can go to for help. Many campuses have an early alert system in place, where individuals can report behavior of an individual for counselors to investigate. Likely, though, you need contact information for that student to allow the report to be pursued. You can, and should, use your professors as resources. They are at the top of the list, as are chairs of departments, deans, counselors, and advisors.

In J.'s case, I was worried about him, so I tried involving First Alert on campus, and nothing prevented his suicide, because nothing could have prevented his suicide. You are not the manager of the act. But talking about loss, crisis, and mental health in our classes is paramount and can enhance our chances to be human.

One of the reasons why this book privileges narrative is because it enforces the validity of disclosure and self-reflection. Self-reflection and awareness of our world and our role in it are assessment tools that can help when and if crisis intervenes in our lives. Narratives for a grade are meant to strengthen writing skills (see Chapter 4 on this). Narratives written during or for class also allow you to disclose information that may be useful for others to know about you. For example, in some of J.'s narrative work, he disclosed his battle with serious depression and how he and his family dealt with it as he grew up. I knew a bit more about him, which contributed to my alarm when he started manifesting as gloomy or upset. He was.

Disclosure is voluntary in writing and also a form of analysis. Reflection itself analyzes a trait, characteristic, or event and makes sense out of it, gives it meaning within a context. This alone is a human necessity to live a fuller life. As a writer, it offers the ability to more deeply understand the pieces of our lives and to communicate what they mean with language. J. liked to write and read—he identified both as a system of comfort and release. This brings me solace because he was thinking through his world and his life as he was living it.

In a clichéd world, writers commit suicide: Sylvia Plath, Virginia Woolf, David Foster Wallace, John Berryman, Ernest Hemingway, and the list keeps going. This doesn't mean writing and creativity cause suicide or depression. Rather, it usually means the writer was leaning on the solace of the creative endeavor of writing to cope with living and any mental disorder or struggle. If writing helps you, keep writing.

Students, when faced with narrative topic choices, often write about a death they've experienced. It is important to distinguish writing and therapy. The practice of writing requires the analysis of the experience—something that those living within active trauma likely may not get to right away. The practice of therapy through writing asks you to write everything and then make sense of it later, even in a new context, like speaking. These are two different modes of communication. As Anne Panning says on the first day of her nonfiction workshop, "Writing for this class is not therapy." She's right. This will save you heartache and time if you understand this concept.

If you experience a death during a semester, you have options. There's a bad practice among professors: to question the veracity of the student's reason for missing class when it's a deceased relative, particularly when it's a grandparent. This stems from professors saying they have heard this excuse for so long that is renders the messenger a liar. Let me be clear on this: if someone has passed away in your family and you need to miss class, you have every right to miss class. If you are doubted, this is not your fault or problem. The death of a loved one is incredibly damaging to an individual; not being believed when a death occurs is untenable.

As discussed in Chapter 5, the documentation required if you attend a funeral is in poor practice: you should not need to get an obituary or a signed document from a funeral parlor to have a class absence excused. If this is happening, go to the chair or the dean, or your advisor or counselor for clarity and help. Some people cannot bear to read the obituary of the one they've lost. This is serious business. Education should not put you in the position of re-mourning or re-traumatizing you due to a death. You are a person who matters.

What came out of the loss of J. in the middle of a semester was the impact it had on the class and on individual students. We took a week off when he died—we called these optional conferences, and students came in when and if they wanted to, to chat with each other or with me. Being in the room where J. was every Monday, Wednesday, and Friday was tough for many. After that week, we resumed class in the room. But I changed the curriculum. I brought guest speakers in who talked about suicide and coping. I brought a career counselor in and we took StrengthsQuest assessments—I wanted students to cherish their strengths and good qualities, especially now.

StrengthsQuest made some students angry, because the rhetoric of this positive psychology informs us that we should only secure occupations that highlight our strengths—some students found this to be restrictive and an easy way out. We talked through this with the facilitator. We returned to writing about ourselves using research and assessments. Students learned more about who they were and what crises might send them spiraling downward. Given the nature of being a college student, you have a lot going on, from family life, to working, to studying, to socializing, to eating, drinking, living, and maintaining the life of a student on a college campus. This is a lot. Assessing your needs on a regular basis might help calm the storm when the storm comes your way.

Richtel also points to the overbearing amount of stress students experience—as a normative, daily way you live. He sees the impact our society's expectations have on your stress levels:

> In addition to whatever overt pressures students feel to succeed, that culture is intensified by something more insidious: a kind of doublespeak from parents and administrators. They often use all the right language about wanting students to be happy, healthy, and resilient—a veritable 'script,' said Madeline Levine, a Bay Area psychologist who treats depressed, anxious, and suicidal tech-industry executives, workers, and their children. They say, 'All

I care about is that you're happy,' and then the kid walks in the door and first question is, 'How did you do on the math test?'

Anxiety is quite common in students' lives—but managing it can be tough. And, as Richtel adds, "the bar for academic success here has become so high that solid performance can feel mediocre. "Here," to the article, means a specific top-tier high school, but here for you means any expectations you feel from family, friends, professors, bosses, and yourself. That anxiety creeps in and often stays with you. Talking to peers in class, and writing about these experiences, can help manage this stress.

Navigating the Storm: Assessing Your Needs

Read through this list, circling the level of each stressor in your world right now.

These stressors have been adapted from *The Chronicle of Higher Education*'s "A Profile of Freshmen at 4-Year Colleges, Fall 2013."

Stressor:	Ranking:		
Self-esteem	Doesn't impact me	Somewhat impacts me	Deeply impacts me
Family Systems	Doesn't impact me	Somewhat impacts me	Deeply impacts me
Grades	Doesn't impact me	Somewhat impacts me	Deeply impacts me
Friends	Doesn't impact me	Somewhat impacts me	Deeply impacts me
Dating	Doesn't impact me	Somewhat impacts me	Deeply impacts me
Drinking	Doesn't impact me	Somewhat impacts me	Deeply impacts me
Drug Use	Doesn't impact me	Somewhat impacts me	Deeply impacts me
Employment (current)	Doesn't impact me	Somewhat impacts me	Deeply impacts me
Future Plans	Doesn't impact me	Somewhat impacts me	Deeply impacts me
Transportation	Doesn't impact me	Somewhat impacts me	Deeply impacts me
Money and Budget	Doesn't impact me	Somewhat impacts me	Deeply impacts me
Children	Doesn't impact me	Somewhat impacts me	Deeply impacts me
Ability to Eat	Doesn't impact me	Somewhat impacts me	Deeply impacts me
Ability to Study	Doesn't impact me	Somewhat impacts me	Deeply impacts me
Management of Mental Health	Doesn't impact me	Somewhat impacts me	Deeply impacts me
Sleeping Patterns	Doesn't impact me	Somewhat impacts me	Deeply impacts me
Racism	Doesn't impact me	Somewhat impacts me	Deeply impacts me
Sexism	Doesn't impact me	Somewhat impacts me	Deeply impacts me

Stressor:	Ranking:		
Ageism	Doesn't impact me	Somewhat impacts me	Deeply impacts me
Ability to Complete Homework	Doesn't impact me	Somewhat impacts me	Deeply impacts me

Add up all the "deeply impacts me" answers and write how many you have here: _____

Add up all the "somewhat impacts me" answers and report that number here: _____

Add up all the "doesn't impact me" answers and report that number here: _____

What do you see?

Write a brief reflective response to these numbers. What is causing the most and least amounts of stress? Why? How can resources be in put in place for help? How can your low impact categories reveal how you manage and deal with potential stressors in a healthy way?

Stress is real and happens. That list looks long, but doesn't cover even half of what is likely causing you stress right now. Issues from running out of money for printing on campus when a paper's due, to transportation struggles, to a bad grade on a test, to a disagreement with a professor, to your work schedule not accommodating your student schedule, are all causes of student stress. That's okay. The idea is not to let stress become your best friend. Many college students let stress accompany them through their years at school—professors expect stress in their classes, students talk about how stressed they are, and the media portrays college as a series of tests and potentials for failure. This does not have to be your life. One test that usually buoys students is the Grit Test, an online tool made by A.L. Duckworth et al., social psychologists who want you to see how tenacious, strong, and capable you are in the face of an obstacle or challenge. Taking this test can help prove that you have areas of clear strength and courage within you (take the test with the link in this chapter's Suggested Materials). The key is to remind yourself that your grit exists and to celebrate your abilities as you move through the rough, rewarding territory of being a student.

As a cautionary tale, in college, I let stress get the best of me, and I stopped eating. Well, I ate root beer barrels (a solid candy) to curb my appetite. It worked for a while. I lost a lot of weight. I started running (which I don't love), and I lost more weight. I got really, really tired. I couldn't really communicate to my roommates about how I felt because, well, everyone was stressed. Many, many college women (and men) control what they can in their chaotic college lives by controlling their eating and drinking—or by letting both get outrageous.

When I went to the dentist, I had something like 17 cavities and an eating disorder in full bloom. Both have stayed with me. The cavities were easier to fix than the disorder—anorexia is chronic. This is not to scare you. It is to say, I get it. The stress of a college student, any part-time or full-time individual invested in coursework, is real. The counselors on campus are wonderful resources—on my campus, the counselors are the advisors, and some are equipped to deal with everything from your course schedule to your depression. On other campuses, advisors are separate from the trained counselors to help with mental health and wellness. No matter what the names are, reach out. Your advisor can advocate for you when and if you need to see a mental health professional. And those people on campus are part of your student fees and available to you. Visit with them.

Other students see your stress the way you see your peers' stress—and stress can manifest in behaviors, tone, voice, and appearance. You can tell when someone you care for is unwell. In a class that feels like a community, you have a set of resources in your fellow students. When J. passed away, the class started eating lunch together when they could. Many came and left class together. They held each other up. Some stayed in touch after the semester ended. Many came to see me. There was not judgment about how they were handling the stress of the grief. They listened, talked, wrote, and dealt with the sorrow.

After a crisis, you need to process. That's why advisors and counselors are so important. So are professors and administrators whom you have gotten to know, and other students on campus, and friends and family. Don't process entirely alone. Some alone time works well. But tipping into isolation can damage your recovery from the event or feeling.

Dan Savage, founder of the "It Gets Better Project," is just one of many off-campus resources to utilize. His project is a series of videos from ordinary people and celebrities explaining that the process of coming out gets better, as does the issue of being bullied for simply being yourself. The campaign has helped thousands of people who didn't know their struggle was someone else's, too. There's also the National Suicide Prevention Hotline (1-800-273-8355), and websites such as the Suicide Prevention Resource Center and the American Foundation for Suicide Prevention that can help you navigate your own, or a classmate's, crisis and recovery.

When I was in graduate school, my dad had a mental breakdown and became suicidal. His house was foreclosed upon, his wife (my mother) left him, and he was using alcohol to cope. When all this happened, I was enrolled in coursework, working as a teaching assistant, and recovering from the trauma of the abusive relationship I had recently left. I had to tell my boss about my father, because I was afraid he would come to my workplace. I felt small, scared, and alone. I was none of these things, because my friends, classmates, and eventual-husband Dan helped me. I had to tell them what was happening. I stayed enrolled in classes because they were a relief to me, a respite from my family chaos. I still admire the professors who helped me, the counselor who saw me and said, "You look tired," and the people on campus who saw stress and acknowledged it in me. I couldn't have coped alone. And you don't have to.

What does stress have to do with writing? Everything. As I heard Ernest Morrell say in his keynote address at Johnson County Community College, what we do in our classrooms and in education is a life and death matter. Enroll and engage in classes where your life matters most, where your research essay is not tantamount to your welfare. Also, we write from where we are. Even if you are writing a research paper, or a cover letter, or a resume, you are writing your life into the pages. You are writing with your current attitude—and that will come through (as we talked about in Chapter 13). If you're unwell, your writing will eventually reveal this. If you are stressed, you may not be able to work as hard as you wanted to on your coursework. What matters is embracing all of this as the experience of being alive—and writing it all down. The narrative portion of your life is ongoing. We tell ourselves our narratives as we walk, eat, think, drive. Our story is always there. Writing it down, making sense of who we are, is a profound exercise in reflective analysis. Once you make meaning from your world and yourself, you grow, and you allow attachments to form and connect to other course material.

You matter. If I have said nothing else of meaning in this book (and you got to Chapter 14—congratulations, that's grit), let this sink in: you matter. Not simply as a student, or a professional, or a mom or dad or friend or loner or manic depressive or athlete, but as you. What you're doing—going to college, or even reading a book about going to college, is huge. You have embraced the idea that you're worth the education, you are worth the courses, the effort, and the thinking. Because you are. If no one is saying this to you, hear it now: You are faced with a nearly impossible task (being a college student and staying alive), and you are doing a good job.

My classes function well when my students function well—and when I am well. When my husband's brother died from heart failure at the start of a fall semester, on his 40th birthday, I fell apart. We had to travel to New York from Kansas and deal with the grief. My husband's brother had died, suddenly. I was a wreck.

When we returned to the semester, I was still a wreck. I went to therapy (and continue to do so). I processed a bit with students and my colleagues. I wrote and wrote—things I will never publish, and some essays that I did publish. Writing was and was not therapy. My published work wasn't therapy, but the journal-writing was. That semester, I rode the commuter bus and, often in the dark after a long day, I tried hard not to cry.

If you've ever tried really hard not to cry, you know what this feels like. If you have never had this experience, you may one day. I was like this when J. died. Nothing made sense. If you have ever experienced death, or when you do, these are normal and healthy reactions. And this is why you cannot, should not, ever let a professor question a death or ask for documentation. When faculty complain about "the third death of a grandmother" that a student tells them about, I remind them that, if the student is, in fact, lying, then that's a really sad, scared person. We need to give each other the trust to believe. I lose the privilege of being an educator when I stop trusting you—especially when you confide in me that someone in your family has died. Take time with this. Stand up for yourself on this. I said it before: education can be a life and death matter.

I encourage you to pay attention to your own feelings, and the behaviors and feelings of those in your classes. Some of the meaningful experiences I have had teaching are the times when I have cried in front of classes. It doesn't happen often, but when it does, it puts me on the level of the student: we are all human. This is not a cliché. When we're entering into territory about school shootings and training for when (not if) a shooting occurs, this is a life and death matter.

I have J.'s First Day Sheet pinned to my bulletin board in my office on campus. I look at it every day. I want to honor the student and person he was to me, and to the community of students in my classes. On the sheet, he identified intelligence as a strength, and as a possible obstacle, he wrote, "coming to class, being held accountable by B." He was held accountable by B. And that series of interactions in class has a life-long foothold in the friendship B. got to have with J. He couldn't save J., but they made each other's lives rich, big, and good.

I think of J. often. I only knew him for two months. This is not what matters. What matters is having a class full of humans who write and think out loud, who laugh and argue, who are so wholly themselves that we care this much. Care this much about each other, and advocate for yourself. Being an educator is a privilege; being your educator is a privilege. Being a student is a unique, awe-inspiring, challenging experience. Ask for help. Use your resources. Write it down. The death of J. is what I could focus on, but I would be missing all the life he gave to us that semester. That's what counts, the light you bring to the world. Keep going. Onward.

©Balazs Kovacs Images/Shutterstock, Inc.

SUGGESTED MATERIALS

American Foundation for Suicide Prevention. afsp.org. Web. 2015.

Link: http://www.afsp.org/

Bell, Sam. "Why Professors Should Give a Damn." *The Chronicle of Higher Education.* chronicle. com. 9 May 2014. Web.

Link: http://chronicle.com/blogs/conversation/2014/05/09/why-professors-should-give-a-damn/

Chronicle of Higher Education. "A Profile of Freshmen at 4-Year Colleges, Fall 2013." *The Chronicle of Higher Education.* chronicle.com 18 Aug. 2014.

Link: http://chronicle.com/article/A-Profile-of-Freshmen-at/147335/

Duckworth, A.L., C. Peterson, M.D. Matthews, and D.R. Kelly. "12-Item Grit Scale." sas.upenn.edu Web. 2007.

   Link: http://www.sas.upenn.edu/~duckwort/images/12-item%20Grit%20Scale.05312011.pdf

Duckworth, A.L., C. Peterson, M.D. Matthews, and D.R. Kelly. "Grit: Perseverance and Passion for Long-Term Goals." *Journal of Personality and Social Psychology* 9 (2007): 1087–1101.

National Suicide Prevention Lifeline. suicidepreventionlifeline.org. Web.

   Link: http://www.suicidepreventionlifeline.org/

Richtel, Matt. "Push, Don't Crush, the Students." *The New York Times Sunday Review*. 26 Apr. 2015. 1, 7.

   Link: http://www.nytimes.com/2015/04/26/sunday-review/push-dont-crush-the-students.html

Savage, Dan. *It Gets Better Project.* itgetsbetter.org. Web. 2010.

   Link: http://www.itgetsbetter.org/

StrengthsQuest. strengthsquest.com. Web. 2010.

   Link: http://www.strengthsquest.com/content/143792/Strengths-Educators.aspx

Suicide Awareness Voices of Education. save.org. Web. 2003.

   Link: http://www.save.org/

Suicide Prevention Resource Center. sprc.org. Web. 1994.

   Link: http://www.sprc.org/

CHAPTER 15

Portfolios and Hearing from the Experts: Educators Weigh In

INTRODUCTION

At the end of the semester, professors in Composition I collect work from you. Sometimes, this is a final paper. A lot of the time, we ask you to collect your best work from the semester and make a **portfolio** out of it. A **portfolio** is a collection of your writing that represents your most advanced, polished writing during the semester, and shows the progress from the beginning, middle, and end of the semester. Usually, the portfolio asks for a **letter of reflection**, or a letter that explains what you included in the portfolio, and why. Usually, students discuss what worked in their writing, what was a struggle or a challenge, and what the professor should really pay attention to when looking at the portfolio. It's the start of a conversation about your work. What you will see in this portfolio section are quotations from many educators. In a single-writer portfolio, like your own, these quotes would all be from writing you have done that showcases your best work and your growth. Here, we'll see a multi-voiced portfolio presenting many people's ideas.

SAM'S REFLECTION

This chapter is a gift. I have made a portfolio out of this chapter by interviewing some of the most impactful educators I have had the privilege of knowing. I interviewed many educators—some are former teachers of mine, some are current colleagues. One is my husband, Dan. All have changed lives by being outstanding educators, and we are lucky they are sharing with us.

This chapter gives me the ability to connect with educators and to give you, the student, insight about professors and advisors, what we struggle with, what we love about teaching and advising, and what might make your lives easier, and more rewarding. The people in this chapter have changed my life and countless others' lives. For you, the gift of this chapter is the advice, the expertise, and the insider knowledge that sometimes is rare to get from professors in college; usually, professors and advisors are asking students the questions. Here, the professors and advisors are answering questions. What is before you now is a portfolio of what these educators said.

On Teaching and Advising: Rewards and Challenges of Being a Professor or Advisor

Particularly for my more advanced class, my goal is to make myself unnecessary, so the most fulfilling moment is when I approach a student in class and ask if they need help and they can honestly answer, 'No, I got this.'

The most challenging thing is when students just disappear—one day they are in class doing fine, and then they are just gone. You don't notice it the first day because everyone has to miss once in a while, but the second and third day that a student isn't there and does not reach out to let you know what is happening, that's a challenge. --- Maureen Fitzpatrick, English Professor, Johnson County Community College

I believe that every student is aspirational. Every student has goals. I would hope working with students was every educator's most fulfilling aspect of the job. Students are the purpose of this process.

Fulfillment is the ability to help students develop the transferable skills that will help them navigate the rest of their lives as autonomous people. --- Dan McCarthy, Academic Advisor, William Allen White School of Journalism and Mass Communications, University of Kansas

The most fulfilling part about teaching is talking to students one-on-one. English teachers get to know their students really well. In Composition I especially we can help get students off to a good start in their college careers.

My most challenging task is managing time in my classroom. I could be a whole lot more structured. --- Dr. Keith Geekie, English Professor and Department Chair, Johnson County Community College

Seeing students grow and develop is the most fulfilling for me. Seeing students grow academically, socially, spiritually, emotionally, etc. is awesome. Growth is something every single student has the opportunity to experience in college, and if they don't, then I feel like we've failed as educators.

I owe it to my students to learn more so I can better serve them. --- Kelli Nichols, former Assistant Dean, William Allen White School of Journalism and Mass Communications, University of Kansas

What is most fulfilling about teaching is seeing students gain confidence in themselves and their writing skills over the course of the semester.

The biggest challenge with teaching is figuring out how to reach every student in the classroom and keep each student engaged in learning. Each student's learning style is so unique, so idiosyncratic, and the skill levels of the students so varied, that developing class activities for everyone is often very difficult. Knowing where the middle ground is in each class, and how to reach it so everyone benefits, is one of my most challenging tasks. --- Joanna McNaney Stein, Lecturer of English, CUNY Kingsborough Community College

The most fulfilling part about teaching is seeing first-generation college students, or those who simply feel excluded or disenfranchised from the experience of higher education, blossom and grow so beautifully, and for them to see their place in the world better and bigger than they'd previously imagined. --- Dr. Anne Panning, English Professor, SUNY Brockport

I like to feel useful to my students. I hate the quantitative side of evaluation. I dislike assigning numbers to my students' work. I don't believe in grades as pedagogical tools. I believe they get in the way of most learning, and they foster the climate that rewards certain kinds of students while turning off others (for reasons that have nothing to do with the student's talent as a thinker, researcher or writer). I still experience grading papers as a soul killing chore.

I find negatively challenging all of the aspects of teaching that reinforce the antagonism between student and teacher. --- Danny Alexander, English Professor, Johnson County Community College

Most challenging to me is the persistent belief (by teachers, students, and pretty much everyone) that writing is useful only to communicate fully formed ideas. That's only, maybe, half of its value. For me, writing is a way of learning, a way of investigating, of figuring out. The way we teach writing—as a tool for persuading or explaining—really just scratches the surface of all the ways writing can—I swear—make us better, kinder, healthier people. --- Ben Stein, Adjunct Professor, English Department, Cleveland State University

I am quite fulfilled by the classroom experience. I almost always enjoy students' company; I like getting to know them personally, their backgrounds, activities, hopes, and dreams. Being both a conduit and a catalyst for my students becoming better readers and writers is deeply satisfying as well.

Most challenging is that many of my students neither read often enough nor well enough and this entails a host of challenges. --- Dr. Michael Valk, Lecturer, English Department, University of Kansas

I love working with students because I get to help. If I'm lucky, I get to be there for the ups and downs, I get to challenge and support, and I learn a lot about myself in the process. Watching a student succeed, no matter the goal, is extremely satisfying.

One semester I had a student that didn't show up to several class sessions and frequently no-showed me for individual appointments. Through email communication, I discovered that this student was dealing with depression and having trouble getting out of bed. Despite multiple attempts to reach out to this student, the semester came to a close, I had to give the student a failing grade, and I never heard from or saw the student again. During my first semester as a resident assistant, a young woman living on my floor took her own life by hanging herself in her residence hall room. Situations like these are, by far, the most challenging things about working with students. Sometimes students make choices and live lives that are beyond our control and sometimes the consequences are negative. I will never be able to sit easy with this reality. --- Sonja "Sony" Heath, Academic Advisor, School of Education, University of Kansas

What is most fulfilling about advising students is the knowledge that you have helped students discover a realistic and satisfying vision of what they want to achieve. What is most fulfilling about teaching is the knowledge that you have shown your students not only something important but also a way toward it and have motivated them to follow that way.

What is most challenging about teaching and advising is students' resistance to being motivated to follow a way toward it. I think successfully encountering that challenge depends a lot on the advisor or the teacher's ability to exemplify the value of what is presented for the students' attention. --- Dr. Michael L. Johnson, retired English Professor and Department Chair, University of Kansas

Regardless of whether the goal is short or long term, I am humbled every semester by getting to learn students' stories and help them figure out how to navigate their past in order to make the best of their future.

The most challenging part of teaching is the student who either does not show up (they don't know what they are missing) or comes every day and chooses not to engage. I can't help anyone who isn't present. --- Amy Pace, Adjunct Professor, English Department, Johnson County Community College

On Student Success: What Educators Want You to Know about Writing and College

A grade is just a way of reflecting back to you my perception of the degree to which you demonstrated a pre-determined set of skills. It's not a reward or punishment, and it's not even a measurement of your writing ability.

What will help you succeed is either (a) knowing exactly what you want from the experience and using that knowledge to help you stay focused and motivated, or (b) knowing that you definitely do not know what you want from the experience, and using that knowledge to inspire openness to new ways of being and excitement about exploring possibilities. I think it's better to be in category (b). I bet Sam does too. But you don't have to listen to either of us. --- Ben Stein, Adjunct Professor, English Department, Cleveland State University

The key to motivation is eagerness to learn. All learning is self-teaching. --- Dr. Michael L. Johnson, retired English Professor and Department Chair, University of Kansas

Your writing (or schooling) past does not define you as a writer and writing is an exercise in thinking, not just executing a grammatical sentence.

Students who are successful in college learn that all learning has to come from a desire to be changed by the learning process. Truly successful people in general understand that 'I don't know' really means 'I can find out.' --- Amy Pace, Adjunct Professor, English Department, Johnson County Community College

I want the least confident students to know they can do it. I want them to know that I don't think of this class as merely academic but, instead, as a uniquely valuable social experience with real life application. I want them to know that I'm on their side and they already have my respect. I often tell my students I got through college by relating everything to my record collection. --- Danny Alexander, English Professor, Johnson County Community College

Try everything people suggest. Try everything once and then try it again. The idea of a single writing process is kind of a lie. You are a complex person who is adapting and learning all the time. --- Maureen Fitzpatrick, English Professor, Johnson County Community College

I always say to my students: Most people regret things they haven't done more than they regret things they've done. Be willing to falter occasionally, but falter proudly and beautifully and you'll be fine. --- Dr. Anne Panning, English Professor, SUNY Brockport

I would like my students to know more about the First Amendment and the tradition of academic freedom. An English class is, or ought to be, a sanctuary where it is safe to explore readings, research, composition and concepts wherever they may lead.

Though students may feel exposed or even institutionally exploited in a 'required' English class, at the same time they are protected by the First Amendment and other laws that make the United States college classroom one of the few places on earth where they do not need to fear retaliation for what they say. Everything they write and read is an exercise of their constitutional prerogatives. An English class, regardless of students' preconceived notions, is a community that participates in the world beyond itself simply by its very existence. A student's struggle toward coherent expression is the struggle of us all and an exercise of those rights that never grow weary from use.

In my limited experience, students succeed who believe education matters; for them it isn't just a chore and an item that they are checking off a list. Students need to take themselves seriously as students, not simply as people taking classes. But the students who succeed the best are those who identify themselves as students, unapologetically. Education will genuinely help them lead their best lives. --- Dr. Keith Geekie, English Professor and Department Chair, Johnson County Community College

Three things help students succeed in college: find your place; ask questions; persevere. (Really, isn't that the same for just being successful in life, too?). There is a place for you. Find your place. Find your people.

I want students to know that what they have to say is important. They deserve to be heard. Written communication can be one very powerful way to let your voice be heard. Fair or not, when you write well you're taken more seriously and voices become more powerful. --- Kelli Nichols, former Assistant Dean, William Allen White School of Journalism and Mass Communications, University of Kansas

You don't have to know where you're going or where you'll end up. You simply have to be ready to start. Oh, and don't compare your writing or your abilities to your peers or friends. In fact, please get out of this habit as soon as possible. Your biggest competition should be yourself.

Don't let college happen to you. Be an active participant. Don't stop asking questions and seeking your own answers. Challenge authority but respect the past. Know that there are so many people here to help you find success and never stop leaning on them for support. --- Sonja "Sony" Heath, Academic Advisor, School of Education, University of Kansas

At the start of a Composition class, I remind my students that writing is not about having perfect grammar or perfect sentence structure or perfect anything. Writing is about generating interesting ideas, and allowing these ideas to grow into something meaningful over time. Most importantly, I tell them writing is about trusting that you have something important and valuable to say to the world, and not being afraid to say it.

What helps students succeed in college is respecting where they have been, where they are at, and encouraging them to do their best work from that place. Having assignments geared towards writing personal narratives helps to achieve this. Their own personal stories matter. --- Joanna McNaney Stein, Lecturer of English, CUNY Kingsborough Community College

The work ahead is serious, a serious adventure, that should excite and expand, first and foremost, students' imaginations. This fosters a sense of possibility. Students should know that they will be considered adults and, most importantly, treated as adults by their teachers . . . fallible, fun-loving adults. --Dr. Michael Valk, Lecturer, English Department, University of Kansas

If you feel a course is superfluous and unnecessary, because it is a general education course, you are implying your self-expression is superfluous and unnecessary. I believe every human has an amazing story, and the diversity of how and why those stories are told is as diverse as the people in the universe. You have to decide how you want to express yourself. --- Dan McCarthy, Academic Advisor, William Allen White School of Journalism and Mass Communications, University of Kansas

FINAL WORDS OF WISDOM FROM AMAZING EDUCATORS

** Listen to these people and what they say. Seriously.

Try to treat college like an amazing privilege, an opportunity to learn things you couldn't learn any-where else, in classes and dorm rooms and dining halls and bookstores and neighborhoods and parks and waiting rooms and cars and everywhere else you go. --- Ben Stein, Adjunct Professor, English Department, Cleveland State University

Students need to be able to imagine their best selves while working away in specific classes. It takes a lot of heart and courage to do that, to have that kind of perspective. They are improving a skill they already possess and will use and improve on in the future. I really do believe then that Composition teachers help students lead better lives. --- Dr. Keith Geekie, English Professor and Department Chair, Johnson County Community College

Don't be afraid of making mistakes. Not even published authors write something perfectly the first time they put their pens to paper. There are great ideas inside of you if you give yourself the time and space to let them loose! --- Joanna McNaney Stein, Lecturer of English, CUNY Kingsborough Community College

The first time you have a reading assignment for any class, set a timer for five minutes. Read while taking notes. When the timer goes off, count the number of pages you have read and multiply it by 12—that's how many pages of psychology you can read in an hour. If your calculation tells you that you can read 45 pages in an hour, that means a 20-page assignment will take you just shy of a half-hour to complete. Schedule that amount of time.

Language and human thought are the two best sets of Lego you can find—you can build anything out of them, so play. We are not that interested in the most obscure words you know or the longest sentences you can create; we care deeply about a great insight presented with clarity. We are not as interested in what your sources say as we are in what your brain does with the information and the ideas. You and your ideas are the stars of your own papers—put that at the center of every project and don't let unnecessary stuff get in the way. --- Maureen Fitzpatrick, English Professor, Johnson County Community College

Your major is not your career. Seriously, your major is not your career. Students have ample time to waste. Students have ample time to explore, as well. The difference is engagement.

To engage is to stop performing and instead explore the fabric of existence. If you believe this is a waste, you may continue to perform your function among your division of labor, but you relinquish the right to ask why you feel so inhuman later in life. --- Dan McCarthy, Academic Advisor, William Allen White School of Journalism and Mass Communications, University of Kansas

Think of writing as a gift to other people. --- Dr. Anne Panning, English Professor, SUNY Brockport

Take advantage of being in a curious and learning-centered environment. There are a number of people here who want to help you. Let them. --- Kelli Nichols, former Assistant Dean, William Allen White School of Journalism and Mass Communications, University of Kansas

Realize that you are creating habits that you will carry with you for the rest of your life. Unfortunately, whether it be procrastination, binge drinking, or poor interpersonal skills, we can't leave our habits in college. Make sure you create habits you are ready to have for the rest of your life. Don't take for granted this amazing community and the many resources to explore your interests and aptitudes. --- Sonja "Sony" Heath, Academic Advisor, School of Education, University of Kansas

I want to say I know why students may have reservations about school. But every class that comes alive for you stays with you for life. It will be some influence on everything you do. There's a magic that takes place when people get together for the sake of learning, but it's the student who really makes it happen. --- Danny Alexander, English Professor, Johnson County Community College

You should know that almost everyone gave me their answers by saying something like, "I don't know if this is what you were looking for," or "I hope I didn't do this wrong," or "These aren't very good, but . . ." These are your educators—these are your people. Educators doubt themselves just as students do. Educators draft and re-draft. We worry, we shift language, we don't always get it right or even close to right. But you, the students, show up—you encourage us, you listen, you nod when we ask, "Does that make sense?" You support us, too. Students are our people. As proof of this, the picture below is Dr. Michael Valk's answers. Look at how drafted they are. And how well-considered the thoughts. Educators care about you and your experiences.

Thank you for reading this book (or parts of it, or for carrying it around in your bag, or for putting it in the corner of your room). You and your story matter. Remember that. I learned that lesson from the two most influential educators of my life: my mother and my father. Together, and apart, they gave me the initial tools for my educational path. In this way, they prepared me to absorb all the wonderful education I have received from so many inspiring educators in my life. I am married to one of them, the one who reminds me every single day that my story matters. I want you to remind yourself of this every single day: your story matters. Write everything down. Move beyond your own blank pages. You've got this.

Onward.

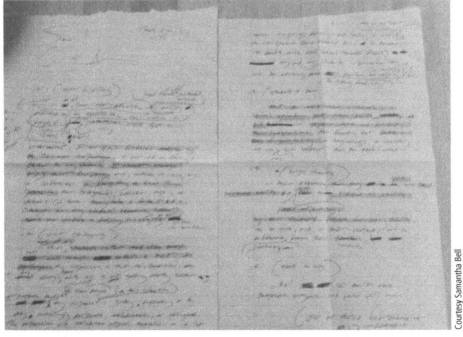

Courtesy Samantha Bell

End-of-Book Assessment

Please answer each question honestly by circling your answer.

I read this book:	YES	NO
This book was useful to me as a college student:	YES	NO
This book was useful to me as a college writer:	YES	NO
I would recommend this book to a friend:	YES	NO
I would recommend this book to an incoming Composition I student:	YES	NO
I would recommend this book to an enemy:	YES	NO
This book should be assigned reading in a Composition I class:	YES	NO

Use the rest of this page to write anything you want. (You have to start somewhere):

Index